Spelling
Made Simple

Stephen V. Ross

Revised by **Sheila Henderson**

Edited and prepared for publication by The Stonesong Press, Inc.

A Made Simple Book
Broadway Books
New York

Edited and prepared for publication by The Stonesong Press, Inc.
Managing Editor: Sheree Bykofsky
Editorial Consultant: Paul Heacock
Design: Blackbirch Graphics, Inc.

Broadway Books titles may be purchased for business or promotional use or for special sales.
For information, please write to: Special Markets Department, Random House, Inc.,
1745 Broadway, New York, NY 10019.

MADE SIMPLE BOOKS and BROADWAY BOOKS are trademarks of Broadway Books,
a division of Random House, Inc.

Visit our website at www.broadwaybooks.com

First Broadway Books trade paperback edition published 2001.

The Library of Congress Cataloging-in-Publication Data has cataloged the Doubleday edition as:
Ross, Stephen V.
    Spelling made simple / Stephen V. Ross:
    revised by Sheila Henderson.
        p.   cm.
    "A Made Simple book."
    1. Spellers.   I. Henderson, Sheila, 1950– .   II. Title.
PE1145.2.R6   1990   89-27150
428.1—dc20   CIP
ISBN 0-385-26642-1

21 20 19

CONTENTS

PART SIX: BECOMING A BETTER WORDSMITH

How to Use This Book

Everyone is capable of correct spelling. Of course, for some it is easier than for others, but correct spelling lies within *everyone's* reach. The key is motivation—and the motivation to spell correctly originates with you. If you sincerely want to become a good speller, *Spelling Made Simple* provides the information, tools, and methods you need to achieve the goal you seek.

Instruction

Thirteen chapters of *Spelling Made Simple* focus exclusively on instruction in the principles governing the English language:

Part I consists of five chapters covering the rules governing most basic spelling situations in American English, as well as the inevitable exceptions to those rules.

Part II consists of three chapters covering the troublesome effects of pronunciation on spelling, including the problems caused by common mispronunciations.

Part III consists of three chapters covering the basic building blocks of language— roots, prefixes, and suffixes—and the ways in which they combine to create different meanings and to serve different functions.

Part IV consists of two chapters covering the tricky rules of punctuation that affect the spelling of many English words.

Four chapters at the end of the book offer instruction in building your vocabulary, learning correct pronunciation, using the dictionary, and developing a powerful memory.

Core Vocabulary

Following each of the thirteen instructional chapters is a special section called the Core Word List. Each Core Word List contains 50 words that are frequently misspelled. The 650 words in the core lists were selected and organized in a sequence that puts the more commonly used words in the earlier Core Word List sections and the less commonly used words in the later sections. *All* the core words are difficult to spell correctly, but those presented in the first several Core Word List sections are *misspelled* most often simply because they are *used* most often. By mastering the correct spelling of these words, you will improve your overall spelling by as much as 75 percent!

Specialized Vocabulary

The eight chapters of Part V are designed specifically to introduce you to words that belong to the specialized vocabularies of various fields of knowledge—from business and law to psychology and religion. This part of the book also includes a chapter covering words and phrases that originated in another language but have come into fairly common use in English. It also includes a chapter covering the correct spelling of commonly used abbreviations. In every chapter except the one on abbreviations, the correct pronunciation of the word is also given.

Practice and Testing

Practice is *essential* to improve your spelling. Both exercises and tests have been included in this book to help sharpen your understanding of the information presented. Each instructional chapter includes practice exercises for every significant section of material covered. The same material is covered in the end-of-chapter mastery tests. The chapters on specialized vocabulary also conclude with mastery tests that examine your understanding of both the spellings and the meanings of these words. Each of the thirteen Core Word List sections concludes with a mastery test covering the words introduced in that section. To help you measure your improvement in spelling, two comprehensive Core Word tests have been included: A pre-test follows this introduction and a post-test follows Chapter 25. Answers to the exercises and tests are included in appendices at the back of the book.

Comprehensive Word List

All words introduced in *Spelling Made Simple*—either in the Core Vocabulary or in the Specialized Vocabulary—are listed alphabetically in a comprehensive word list at the back of the book. This list can serve as a quick reference guide when you want to verify the spelling of a word that you have studied in this book.

Pronunciation Key

A number of chapters in this book provide pronunciation guides for the words contained therein. These pronunciation guides follow a simple system of phonetic respelling. Familiarize yourself with this key and refer back to it whenever you are unclear about a pronunciation.

Vowel Sounds

Vowel sounds are indicated through vowel-vowel and vowel-consonant combinations.

Sound Symbol	Sample Word	Phonetic Spelling
EE	team	TEEM
AY	freight	FRAYT
Y	buy	BY
OH	no	NOH
OO	look	LOOK
EW	cruise	KREWZ
AW	taught	TAWT
AH	farm	FAHRM
UR	fern	FURN
OY	toy	TOY
OW	house	HOWS
YEW	use	YEWZ
I	seive	SIV
A	bat	BAT
E	end	END
O	hot	HOT (This sound varies from short AH to short AW.)
U	cup	KUP

The vowels of unaccented syllables are weak and have only part of the quality of the original or else are completely blurred or indeterminate in quality. For these, the original spellings are usually retained — for example, alone (a-LOHN), system (SIS-tem), easily (EE-zi-lee), honor (ON-or), campus (KAM-pus).

Consonant Sounds

These letters have their usual sound: **b, d, f, h, k, l, m, n, p, r, s, t, v, w, y** (before vowels, as in **yes**), and **z**. The remaining consonants are indicated as follows:

Sound Symbol	Sample Word	Phonetic Spelling
G	ghost	GOHST
J	trudge	TRUHJ
TCH	chief	TCHEEF
NG	sing	SING
SH	sure	SHUR
ZH	measure	MEZH-ur
TH	thin	THIN
T̶H̶	than	T̶H̶AN
KW	quick	KWIK
GZ	exact	EG-zact
KS	complex	COM-pleks

W is used for words spelled with **wh**, since this sound may be a W, a voiceless W, or an HW.

Syllables and Accents

Syllables are separated by dashes—for example, finger (FIN-ger). The syllable that receives the primary accent is indicated by all capital letters—for example, going (GOH-ing), demoniacal (dee-mo-NY-a-kal). The secondary accent is not indicated because it usually does not present a problem.

Core Word Pre-Test

Circle the correctly spelled word(s) in each of the following groups.

1. loseing, losing, lossing
2. proceed, procede, proseed, prosede
3. hieght, heighth, height, hieghth
4. oppinion, opinion, opinnion, oppinnion
5. writing, writeing, writting, writteing

6. proffessor, profesor, proffesor, professor
7. therefor, therefore, therfor, therfore
8. foriegn, forein, forien, foreign
9. marraige, marridge, marriage, marrage
10. all right, alright, allright, all rite
11. heros, heroez, heroes, herroes
12. refered, referred, reffered, refferred
13. amachoor, amatoor, amatuer, amateur
14. atheist, athiest, atheast, athaest
15. ninty, ninety, ninedy, ninnety
16. advertisement, advertizment, advertisment, advertizement
17. leasure, leesure, leisure, liesure
18. labratory, laborattory, laboratory, labaratory
19. irestistible, irresistable, irresistible, iresistible
20. discription, description, descripttion, discripttion
21. efficeint, eficient, eficeint, efficient
22. rhythm, rythm, ryrhm, rhytm
23. embarass, embarrass, emberress, emmbarass
24. enviroment, environent, environment, envirronment
25. exaggerate, exagerate, exagerrate, exegarrate
26. prevalent, privelant, preveland, prevelent
27. irrevelant, irrelevant, irrelevent, irelevant
28. ocurence, occurance, occurence, occurrence
29. accidently, accidentaly, accidentally, accidentilly
30. adolesence, adolecense, adolesense, adolescence
31. wierd, weard, weird, weiard
32. advantagous, advantageous, advanttagous, addvantageous
33. paralel, parralel, parallel, paralell
34. imediately, imeddiately, immediately, immediatly
35. beneficcial, benefficial, beneficail, beneficial
36. criticism, criticizm, critticism, critticizm
37. occassion, occasion, ocassion, ocasion
38. lonliness, lonelyness, loneliness, lonlyness
39. charcteristic, chrackteristic, characteristic, characteristick
40. beleif, beleaf, belief, bellief
41. acomodate, accomadate, acommodate, accommodate
42. dissapoint, disappoint, dissappoint, disapoint
43. grammer, gramar, grammar, gramer
44. athelete, atlete, athleet, athlete
45. intrest, interest, interrest, intirest
46. controversial, contraversial, controversail, contriversial
47. separite, seperate, separate, sepparate
48. maintainance, maintenance, maintenence, maintainence
49. arguement, argumment, argument, arrgument
50. villein, villain, villian, villin

PART ONE

PICKING UP THE BASIC RULES

CHAPTER ONE

EI and IE; AI and IA; -SEDE, -CEED, and -CEDE

EI and IE

You probably remember the rhyming jingle used to teach this spelling rule:

Use **i** before **e** when sounded as **ee**,
Except after **c**,
Or when sounded like **a**,
As in **neighbor** and **weigh**.

Maybe you also remember getting discouraged when this jingle didn't give you the solution for *every* word with an **ei/ie** spelling. There are other **ei/ie** spelling tips you can learn to help you handle this pesky spelling problem—and we'll cover them later in this chapter. But first, let's look a little more closely at the three basic rules in the jingle:

Rule 1: Use **i** before **e**, when sounded as **ee** (long **e** as in **meet**). Here are some typical examples:

IE Pronounced as Long E

achieve	field	reprieve
shield	believe	fierce
brief	shriek	grief
cashier	piece	yield
thief	niece	chief
siege	wield	pierce
relief	retrieve	hygiene

Exceptions to Rule 1: All spelling rules seem to have exceptions, and that's true of the **ei/ie** rules as well. For instance, certain words use **ei** spelling even though they are pronounced with the **ee** sound. Originally, these words were pronounced differently—with a long **a**, a long **i**, or a short **i** sound—and were spelled according to the rules for that pronunciation. Over the years the pronunciation changed, but the spelling didn't.

Here's a list of these "exceptional" words:

either	seize/seizure
neither	weird
leisure	sheik

Rule 2: Use **e** before **i** after the letter **c** (even when sounded as long **e**). Here are some typical examples:

EI After C

ceiling	deceit
perceive	deceive
conceit	receive
conceive	receipt

Rule 3: Use **e** before **i** when sounded like a long **a** (as in **hay**). Here are some typical examples:

EI Pronounced as Long A

neighbor	weigh	freight
neigh	weight	vein
reign	veil	sleigh
rein	skein	deign
eight	feint	surveillance

Some exceptions to rules are important enough to have rules of their own. This is the case with Rule 2: The "except after **c**" rule doesn't apply if the **c** is sounded as **sh**. Here's the "exceptional" rule:

Rule 4: Use **i** before **e** after a **sh** sound. In words of this kind, the **i** pairs with a **c** or **t** to make the **sh** sound, leaving the unaccented **e** (a short **e**, as in **item**) on its own. Here are some typical examples:

IE After SH Sound

sufficient	ancient	deficient
quotient	species	glacier
patient	proficient	conscience

So far, the **ei/ie** spelling rules have covered three different pronunciations of these letter combinations: **ee** as in **meet**, **a** as in **hay**, and **eh** as in **item**. Let's look at how other pronunciations affect the spelling rules.

Rule 5: Use **ei** when sounded as short **i** (as in **hit**). Here some examples:

EI Pronounced as Short I

counterfeit	heifer
foreign	surfeit
sovereign	forfeit

Exceptions to Rule 5: sieve, mischief, mischievous, handkerchief.

Rule 6: Use **ei** when sounded as long **i** (as in **ice**). Here are some examples:

EI Pronounced as Long I

height	sleight
eider	stein
kaleidoscope	seismograph

Two **ie** words don't fall under any of these rules: *friend* (in which the **ie** is sounded as the **e** in **end**) and *financier* (in which the **ie** is sounded as the **ea** in **fear**).

In many of the spelling words introduced in this chapter, **i** and **e** form a *digraph*—that is, the two letters are used to represent a single sound. However, when the **i** and the **e** are pronounced as *separate sounds*, then none of these **ei/ie** spelling rules apply. Instead, you must follow the all-important general rule of spelling: Pay careful attention to pronunciation. Here are examples of **ie/ei** words that *aren't digraphs:*

fiery	clothier	experience
science	sobriety	audience
deity	alien	hierarchy
quiet	society	notoriety

Before we cover the other spelling rules in this chapter, let's test your skill with the rules governing **ei/ie**.

Exercise 1.1

Complete the following words by filling in **ie** or **ei** in the blank spaces.

1. misch_____f-maker
2. pagan d_____ty
3. human spec_____s
4. vitamin defic_____ncy
5. intelligence quot_____nt
6. frozen glac_____r
7. guilty consc_____nce
8. trans_____nt hotel
9. for_____gn agent
10. signed rec_____pt
11. wealthy financ_____r
12. shocked into sobr_____ty
13. shr_____k with rage
14. v_____led reference
15. s_____ze the day
16. good n_____ghbor
17. r_____ns and bridle
18. counterf_____t money
19. l_____sure time
20. dec_____tful lie

AI and IA

The spelling rules for **ai/ia** words are very simple compared to those for **ei/ie** words. In fact, you need to know only three rules to be a good speller of these words.

Rule 1: Use **a** before **i** when sounded as **eh**. When the **a** and **i** make a single sound—in other words, when they form a digraph—then the **a** always comes first. Here are some examples:

AI Pronounced as EH

villain	chieftain
captain	Britain
certain	mountain

Rule 2: Use **i** before **a** when sounded as **uh** or **yuh**. Here are some examples:

IA Pronounced as UH or YUH

civilian	peculiar
familiar	partial
auxiliary	brilliant
financial	genial
Christian	beneficial

Rule 3: Use **i** before **a** when the letters are pronounced separately. Here are a few examples: median, guardian, genial.

Before you learn about spelling words ending in **-sede**, **-ceed**, and **-cede**, test your grasp of the rules governing **ai/ia**.

Exercise 1.2

Complete the following words by filling in **ai** or **ia** in the blank spaces.

1. civil_____n duties
2. wicked vill_____n
3. rocky mount_____n
4. guard_____n angel
5. mart_____l arts
6. auxil_____ry power
7. Christ_____n martyr
8. benefic_____l circumstances
9. tribal chieft_____n
10. cert_____n death

11. Great Brit_____n
12. gen_____l companion
13. pecul_____r habit
14. part_____l solution
15. brill_____nt diamond

-SEDE, -CEED, and -CEDE

English has only twelve words ending with the "seed" pronunciation, and yet they cause nagging spelling problems for many people. These words are all derived from the Latin root **ced** [**cedere**, "to yield"], so each has the idea of yielding in its definition. Since there are so few of these words, the simplest way of learning which spelling to use is *memorization*.

○ **-SEDE**: Only one word in English ends in **-sede**.
   supersede
○ **-CEED**: Only three words in English end in **-ceed**.
   exceed   proceed   succeed
○ **-CEDE**: The remaining eight words that end with the sound "seed" all have the **-cede** spelling.

accede	intercede
antecede	precede
cede	recede
concede	secede

If these words aren't in your vocabulary, look them up and learn their meanings. All of these words are verbs. When they are changed into nouns and adjectives, most of them follow this spelling rule: Change **-ceed** and **-cede** to **-cess**. Note these examples:

proceed	pro**cess**
exceed	ex**cess**ive
succeed	suc**cess**, suc**cess**ive, suc**cess**ion

accede	ac**cess**ion
concede	con**cess**ion
recede	re**cess**, re**cess**ive, re**cess**ion
secede	se**cess**ion

In a few cases, the spelling simply changes to **-ced**:

proceed	pro**ced**ure
antecede	ante**ced**ent

Now test your skill spelling words ending in **-sede**, **-ceed**, and **-cede** and the other words derived from them.

Exercise 1.3

Complete the following words by filling the blank spaces with **-sede**, **-ceed**, **-cede**, **-ced**, or **-cess**.

1. ex_____ the speed limit
2. the correct pro_____ure
3. the pre_____ing day
4. a huge suc_____
5. historical ante_____ent
6. divine inter_____ion
7. con_____ defeat
8. the rush report super_____s
9. inter_____ on his behalf
10. se_____ from the union

Chapter Mastery Test

Review the spelling rules you have learned in this chapter covering **ei/ie**, **ai/ia**, and **-sede**, **-ceed**, **-cede**. Then complete the following questions to test your mastery of these spelling skills.

Part I: Circle or underline the *one* correctly spelled word in each of these word groups.

1. civilain   civilian   civillian
2. succeed   sucede   succede
3. perceive   preceive   percieve
4. beneficial   beneficail   beneficial
5. patiant   pateint   patient
6. intersede   interseed   intercede
7. notoraity   notoriety   notorety
8. proceedure   procedure   procedeure
9. exceed   excede   exseed
10. chieftian   chieftain   cheiftain
11. sheik   shaik   shiek
12. villein   villian   villain
13. omniescence   omnisceince   omniscience
14. prosede   procede   proceed
15. inveigh   invaigh   inviagh
16. preceed   precede   presede
17. sleight   slieght   sleigt
18. antecedent   anteceedent   antesedent
19. supercede   superceed   supersede
20. Christian   Christain   Christien

Part II: Circle the correctly spelled choice in each of these sentences.

1. The German shepherd had a [feirce] [fierce] bark.

2. His grades are [deficient] [deficeint] in geometry and biology.

3. The con man fooled people with his [gienial] [genial] smile.

4. People who prepare food must have good [hygiene] [hygein].

5. She had a [peculair] [peculiar] expression on her face.

6. Prince Ralph is third in [sucession] [succession] to the throne.

7. He hid his [conciet] [conceit] behind a mask of humility.

8. I see a [foriegn] [foreign] substance floating in my soup!

9. The tour begins in [Britain] [Britian] and ends in Germany.

10. To [acheive] [achieve], one first must attempt.

Core Word List #1

accommodate	criticism	existent	occurred	separation
achieve	criticize	forty	occurrence	their
achievement	define	fourth	occurring	there
affect	definite	it's	personal	they're
all right	definitely	its	personnel	to
belief	definition	loose	realize	too
believe	effect	lose	really	two
business	effective	losing	receive	weather
busy	exist	occasion	receiving	whether
choose	existence	occur	separate	women
chose				

Core Word Mastery Test

Master the spelling of these words from the core list and learn their meanings before you try to learn those in the chapters ahead. **Remember:** *In spelling, your goal is a perfect score.*

Part I: In the space provided, write the correct choice for each sentence below. Note that although many of the choices are correctly spelled for some sentences, only one is appropriate *in context.*

1. There, at the end of the rainbow—_____ a pot of gold.
   (its, it's, its')
2. Men _____ play important roles in family life.
   (too, two, to)
3. You say _____ coming, but are they?
   (their, they're, there)
4. Why so much ado about so little _____ do?
   (to, too, two)
5. Look _____! The unicorn has lost its horn.
   (there, their, they're)
6. _____ conductivity that makes copper useful for wire.
   (It's, Its', Its)
7. Don't _____ interest; the plot becomes more absorbing as you go on.
   (loose, lose)
8. St. Louis finished _____ in the National League that year.
   (fourth, forth)
9. _____, how can you dislike caviar?
   (Really, Realy, Reely)

10. Ruth could not bear _____ from Naomi.
    (separation, seperation, separetion)
11. We shall attend the lawn party _____ the _____ is pleasant or not.
    (weather, whether, wether)
12. When he offered me two alternatives, I _____ the second of them. Which would you _____?
    (chose, choosed, choose)
13. Why is your choice more _____?
    (affective, effective, efective)
14. What may _____ you need have no _____ upon me.
    (affect, afect, effect)
15. I have a _____ interest in the man the _____ director is considering for that new job.
    (personnal, personnel, personal)
16. Oh men, oh _____!
    (wimmin, woman, women)
17. We need a _____ plan of study aimed at eliminating errors.
    (deffinite, definate, definite)
18. Many naturally _____ disasters negatively affect the environment.
    (occurring, ocurring, occuring)
19. Do you have faith in the _____ of God?
    (exsistence, existence, existance)
20. He has any number of mistaken _____.
    (beleifs, beliefs, belliefs)

Part II: Each of the core list words in the following sentences either *needs an addi-*

tional letter or *has an extra letter*. In either case, correct the spelling.

1. After forty days it occured to Noah that he and his shipmates had reached their destination.
2. In an atomic era man's exsistence often seems to lose its significance.
3. Joe's busness is all right, but he is losing his hair anyhow.
4. Do you really believe that you can accomodate both customers and cousins?
5. I want you two believe that because it is true.
6. Fourty parties in two months will keep any bachelor busy.
7. May I take this ocasion to criticize your achievement?
8. Definitly! I really welcome criticism.
9. Your deffinition of beauty is open to criticism on two counts.
10. Separate those two brawlers and ask them too leave.

Part III: Circle the *one* correctly spelled choice in each of the following sentences.

1. Aaron predicted that the revolution would [occur] [occurr] on schedule.
2. Belial fought a [loseing] [losing] battle against the heavenly host.
3. Citron loved to [receive] [recieve] crab apples for his birthday.
4. Diomedes did not [beleave] [believe] that Hector could outfight him.
5. Ezekiel kept [buzy] [busy] counting bones in Desert Valley.
6. Franchot is handsome, [all right] [alright].
7. Geoffrey's finest [achievement] [achievment] is not in mathematics.
8. Hildegarde never could [seperate] [separate] the men from the boys.
9. Irving disliked personal [criticism] [critisism].
10. James did not [realize] [realise] the absurdity of his argument.

CHAPTER TWO

Final E and Final Y

Final E

A final **e** causes problems because sometimes it is *dropped* when a suffix is added to the word and sometimes it is *kept*. Two rules will help you solve most of these problems.

Rule 1: Drop the final silent **e** before a suffix that begins with a vowel. The most common suffixes that begin with a vowel are **-ed**, **-er**, **-est**, **-ing**, **-able/-ible**, **-ance/-ence**, **-ity**. Less commonly used suffixes include **-ous** and **-age**. Study these examples:

Drop the final **e** before **-ed**:

argue	argu**ed**
change	chang**ed**

Drop the final **e** before **-er**:

write	writ**er**
love	lov**er**

Drop the final **e** before **-est**:

large	larg**est**
fine	fin**est**

Drop the final **e** before **-ing**:

judge	judg**ing**
dine	din**ing**

Drop the final **e** before **-able/-ible**:

conceive	conceiv**able**
value	valu**able**
force	forc**ible**

Drop the final **e** before **-ance/-ence**:

grieve	griev**ance**
confide	confid**ence**

Drop the final **e** before **-ity**:

sincere	sincer**ity**
divine	divin**ity**

Drop the final **e** before **-ous**:

desire   desir**ous**

Drop the final **e** before **-age**:

use   us**age**

Rule 2: Keep the final silent **e** before a suffix that begins with a consonant. The suffixes that begin with a consonant are **-ly**, **-ness**, **-ment**, **-ful**, and **-less**. Study this list of examples:

Keep the final **e** before **-ly**:

complete   complete**ly**
definite   definite**ly**

Keep the final **e** before **-ness**:

polite   polite**ness**
white   white**ness**

Keep the final **e** before **-ment**:

arrange   arrange**ment**
achieve   achieve**ment**

Keep the final **e** before **-ful**:

hope   hope**ful**
grace   grace**ful**

Keep the final **e** before **-less**:

care   care**less**
taste   taste**less**

Unfortunately, these two rules don't cover every situation with the final silent **e**. As with so many other spelling rules, there are some important exceptions. These exceptions assure that certain words won't be mispronounced or mistaken for other words with similar spellings.

Rule 3: Keep the final **e** in words ending in **-ee** and **-oe**. Look at these examples:

see   seeing
agree   agreement
guarantee   guaranteeable
canoe   canoeing
woe   woeful

Rule 4: Keep the final silent **e** before the suffix **-ing** to avoid mispronunciation or ambiguity with certain words. There are only a few words that fall under this rule:

singe ("to scorch")   singeing
(not to be confused with **singing** a song)

dye ("to color")   dyeing
(not to be confused with **dying** of an illness)

Rule 5: Keep the final silent **e** in words ending with **-ce** or **-ge** that have suffixes beginning with **a** or **o**. These words are pronounced with the sound of the **soft c** (as in **fancy**) or the **soft g** (as in **range**). Keeping the **e** before the suffix maintains the soft pronunciation. For instance, without the softening effect of the silent **e**, the word **peaceable** would rhyme with "seekable," the word **changeable** would rhyme with "hangable," and so forth.

peace	peac**eable**
change	chang**eable**
service	servic**eable**
notice	notic**eable**
manage	manag**eable**
advantage	advantag**eous**
courage	courag**eous**
outrage	outrag**eous**

Rule 6: Drop the final **e** after the letters **u** or **w**. Again, only a few words fall under this rule:

true	tru**ly**
due	du**ly**
argue	argu**ment**
awe	aw**ful**

One more small exception: The final silent **e** in **whole** is dropped when the suffix **-ly** is added—**wholly**.

Before you learn the spelling rules covering final **y**, let's test your skill with final **e**.

Exercise 2.1

Complete the spelling of the following words by filling in **e** where necessary. If no **e** is needed, leave the space blank.

1. dy____ing her hair
2. judg____ing the contest
3. to____ing the line
4. heated argu____ment
5. lov____ly day
6. sing____ing the shirt
7. cano____ing trip
8. advantag____ous position
9. grac____ful dancer
10. pursu____ing rainbows
11. strong lik____lihood
12. desir____able property
13. chang____able mood
14. very tru____ly yours
15. most definit____ly
16. dy____ing of boredom
17. aw____ful accident
18. servic____able machine
19. good us____age
20. din____ing car

Final Y

As with the final **e**, there are two main rules about handling the final **y**—with several additional rules that cover exceptions.

Rule 1: Keep the final **y** if it follows a vowel. Here are some examples:

day	d**ays**
attorney	attorn**eys**
annoy	anno**ys**
convey	conve**ys**
employ	emplo**yer**
play	pla**yer**
journey	journ**eyed**
enjoy	enj**oyed**
buy	bu**ying**
relay	rel**aying**

A few words with irregular spellings are important exceptions to this rule:

day	da**ily**
say	sa**id**
pay	pa**id**
lay	la**id**

Rule 2: Change the final **y** to **i** if it follows a consonant or **qu**. Look at these examples:

grassy	grass**ier**
silly	sill**ier**
corny	cor**niest**
ugly	ug**liest**
baby	ba**bies**
country	count**ries**
bury	bu**ries**
satisfy	satis**fies**
reply	rep**lied**
try	**tried**
beauty	beau**tiful**
mercy	mer**ciful**
busy	bu**siness**
lonely	lone**liness**
mystery	myste**rious**
study	stu**dious**
marry	mar**riage**
carry	car**riage**
easy	ea**sily**
clumsy	clum**sily**
rely	re**liance**
defy	de**fiance**
soliloquy	solilo**quies**

Rule 3: Keep the final **y**—even when it follows a consonant—if the suffix is **-ing.** Here are a few examples:

bury	bury**ing**
carry	carry**ing**
rely	rely**ing**
hurry	hurry**ing**

Rule 4: In particular words, keep the final **y** if the suffix is **-ment, -ness,** or **-ful.**

employ	employ**ment**
enjoy	enjoy**ment**
shy	shy**ness**
dry	dry**ness**
sly	sly**ness**
coy	coy**ness**

play	play**ful**
joy	joy**ful**

Now let's test your skill spelling words that end with **y.**

Exercise 2.2

Complete the spelling of the following words by filling in the blank space with **-y-, -i-,** or **-ie-.**

1. la____d to rest
2. happy famil____s
3. eas____ly influenced
4. hidden valle____s
5. self-rel____ance
6. goof____est smile
7. cr____s of sorrow
8. pla____ed in the band
9. myster____ous noises
10. arranged marr____age
11. hurr____d away
12. merc____ful heavens
13. da____ly newspaper
14. big bus____ness
15. anno____ed with himself
16. bur____s the bone
17. long journe____s
18. desert dr____ness
19. rel____s on donations
20. a bevy of beaut____s

Chapter Mastery Test

Review the spelling rules you have learned in this chapter covering final **e** and final **y.** Then complete the following questions to test your mastery of these spelling skills.

Part I: In each of the following groups of words, circle the *one* in which the final **y** is *not* changed or dropped when **-s** is added.

1. satisfy	turkey	country
2. employ	copy	try
3. baby	mercy	relay
4. chimney	bury	hurry
5. convey	pity	injury

Part II: In each of the following groups of words, circle the *one* in which the final **e** is *not* dropped when **-ing** is added.

1. pursue	shoe	admire
2. guarantee	become	move
3. value	service	eye
4. conceive	singe	force
5. decree	amuse	whine

Part III: In the space provided, correctly spell the words formed from the following root words and suffixes.

1. move	+ able	=	_____
2. fine	+ est	=	_____
3. carry	+ ing	=	_____
4. clumsy	+ ly	=	_____
5. manage	+ ment	=	_____
6. taste	+ less	=	_____
7. defy	+ ance	=	_____
8. study	+ ous	=	_____
9. true	+ ly	=	_____
10. advantage	+ ous	=	_____
11. envy	+ ous	=	_____
12. woe	+ ful	=	_____
13. deny	+ ing	=	_____
14. pay	+ ed	=	_____
15. polite	+ ness	=	_____
16. divine	+ ity	=	_____
17. love	+ able	=	_____
18. sassy	+ er	=	_____
19. sure	+ ly	=	_____
20. arrange	+ ment	=	_____

Core Word List #2

acquaint	benefited	exaggerate	loneliness	similar
acquaintance	choice	experience	marriage	surprise
among	comparative	government	necessary	than
athlete	condemn	governor	noticeable	then
athletic	conscientious	immediately	perform	thorough
began	conscious	incidentally	performance	woman
begin	controversial	intelligent	possession	write
beginning	description	interest	prejudice	writer
beneficial	disastrous	interpret	privilege	writing
benefit	environment	interpretation	shining	written

Core Word Mastery Test

Master the spelling of these words from the core list and learn their meanings before you try to learn those in the chapters ahead. **Remember:** *In spelling, your goal is a perfect score.*

Part I: One word in each of the following sentences has a blank space for *one* letter. If a letter should be added to make the spelling correct, add it. If the word is correct as is, ignore the blank space and leave the word as is.

1. Vera has writ_____en her autobiography.
2. Ulysses won many ath_____letic events.
3. Thomas arrived early for Winnie's su_____prise party.
4. Stephen took little int_____rest in girls until he was five years old.
5. Randy has a shin_____ing light in her eyes since Clem proposed.
6. Quincy inherited his father's interest in affairs of gover_____ment.
7. Percy's enviro_____ment encouraged him to develop artistic tastes.
8. Oliver owned a yacht simil_____ar to Percival's.
9. Newton searched for an apple amo_____ng his miscellaneous notebooks.
10. Melissa is begin_____ing to resemble her father, but she may outgrow it.

Part II: Circle the correctly spelled word choices in each of the following sentences.

1. The [governor] [governer] of the state put in [writting] [writing] his approval of the new industrial plant.
2. What [interpretation] [interpertation] of the law compels you to [condem] [condemn] an innocent man?
3. [Marraige] [Marriage] proves [beneficial] [benefical] to some, [disastrous] [disasterous] to others.
4. Before I vote for the new expressway, I should like to make a [through] [thorough] investigation of the expenditures involved.
5. What possible [benifit] [benefit] will you gain from quitting your job?
6. Leonard has no [prejudice] [perjudice] toward foreigners.
7. Maximilian has an [inteligent] [intelligent] approach to financial problems—he neither lends nor borrows.
8. Nestor loved to recall his [experience] [experiance] as a warrior.
9. Oliphant was a [conscientous] [conscientious] worker who gave more to his job than was called for.
10. Franz Ferdinand's morganatic marriage became a [contraversial] [controversial] issue upon which many opinions were voiced.
11. Queequeg developed more than a casual [acquaintance] [acquaintence] with Ishmael.
12. Raskolnikov's [performance] [performence] with an axe left little to be desired.
13. Sylvia gave a vivid [descripion] [description] of the murderer's apparel.
14. Timothy may have been a [comparitive] [comparative] newcomer, but his talents were undeniable.
15. Uriah heaped lavish attention upon his parakeet, but could never get it to [preform] [perform].

Part III: One of the core words in each of the following sentences needs an *extra* letter to make it correct. Add the necessary letter.

1. Advertisers who exagerate the worth of their products deserve to be punished.
2. Immediatly after the party Luella returned to her garret.
3. I should like, incidentaly, to add one more point to my argument.
4. His head is scarcely noticable between his ears.
5. Rank has its privlege, but I have no rank.
6. A toy gun was found in the posession of the youthful burglar.
7. May I aquaint you with the facts of life?
8. I am barely concious of any events going on about me.
9. To escape lonliness many people seek the company of other lonely souls.
10. Is it necesary always to shout in my presence?

Part IV: Proofread the following paragraph, correcting all spelling errors.

Then the athelete began to write. He knew that during this examination he would have to begin to interpet his material. The chooice of one strand of evidence rather then another would reveal whether he had benefitted from his teacher's efforts to show him how to think and writte.

Final Consonants

Remembering when to double a final consonant—and when *not* to—can save you a great deal of misunderstanding and embarrassment. Look at the following sets of similar words. The difference between the correct meaning and disaster is a *single letter!*

fill	**filling** a glass of wine
file	**filing** letters into folders
rid	**ridding** the dog of fleas
ride	**riding** a camel
plan	**planning** a trip
plane	**planing** the edge of the board
mop	**mopping** the floor
mope	**moping** about not getting a raise
wag	**wagging** a finger
wage	**waging** a battle
grip	**gripping** the steering wheel
gripe	**griping** about the weather

From these examples, you can probably figure out the basic guidelines for doubling the consonant at the end of a one-syllable word. Here is the rule that applies:

Rule 1: Double the final consonant in a **one-syllable** word when:

- it stands alone (**dub** but not **dump**);
- it follows a single vowel (**hop** but not **heap**); and
- it is followed by a suffix beginning with a vowel (**shipp<u>ed</u>** but not **ship<u>ment</u>**).

Here's a sampler of one-syllable words whose final consonants are doubled:

beg	beg**gar**, beg**ged**, beg**ging**
brag	brag**gart**, brag**ged**, brag**ging**
rob	rob**ber**, rob**bed**, rob**bing**
quit	quit**ter**, quit**ting**
drug	drug**gist**, drug**ged**, drug**ging**

cram   crammed,
                cramming
drop   dropped, dropping
man   manned, manning
stab   stabbed, stabbing
whip   whipped,
                whipping

Of course, as with almost all spelling rules, there are a few exceptions to this general rule. Here are a few of them:

row   rowing
gas   gaseous

Do this quick exercise to test your understanding of this rule.

Exercise 3.1

Correctly spell the words formed from the following root words and endings in the space provided.

1. bar   + ing   = _____
2. croak   + ed   = _____
3. look   + ing   = _____
4. mow   + er   = _____
5. scrub   + ed   = _____
6. mix   + ing   = _____
7. cram   + ed   = _____
8. hurt   + ing   = _____
9. pot   + ed   = _____
10. moan   + ing   = _____

Rule 2: Double a final consonant in a **multi-syllable** word when:

o it stands alone (**defer** but not **design**);
o it follows a single vowel (**regret** but not **retreat**);
o it is followed by a suffix beginning with a vowel (**occurrence** but not **annulment**); and
o it is in a multi-syllable word that is accented on the last syllable (**omit** but not **benefit**).

Here are various examples of words that fall under this rule:

begin   beginner, beginning
permit   permitted, permitting
transfer   transferred, transferring
aquit   acquitted, acquittal
rebel   rebelled, rebellion
abhor   abhorring, abhorrence
admit   admitted, admittance
excel   excellent, excellence
forbid   forbidden, forbidding

Note that in certain words the accent shifts to the first syllable when the suffix is added. In these cases, the consonant does not double. Here are some examples:

confer   conferring   conference
defer   deferring   deference
infer   inferring   inference
refer   referring   reference

Check your understanding of this rule by completing the following exercise.

Exercise 3.2

Correctly spell the words formed from the following root words and endings in the space provided.

1.	infer	+ ing	= _____
2.	amend	+ ing	= _____
3.	conceal	+ ment	= _____
4.	equip	+ age	= _____
5.	quarrel	+ ed	= _____
6.	repel	+ ent	= _____
7.	exist	+ ence	= _____
8.	transmit	+ er	= _____
9.	consider	+ ing	= _____
10.	legal	+ ize	= _____

An additional rule about final consonants applies to special situations with suffixes:

Rule 3: When the suffix begins with the same consonant that the word ends with, use both consonants—even though doing so appears to violate other rules about doubling final consonants. Here are some examples of these special situations:

mean	mea**nn**ess
thin	thi**nn**ess
careful	carefu**ll**y
wonderful	wonderfu**ll**y

One final rule applies to words that end with a **c**. Although you shouldn't double the final consonant in these words, you *should* add another consonant to make sure the pronunciation remains proper.

Rule 4: Add **k** to words ending in **c** before suffixes beginning with **e**, **i**, or **y**. Putting the **k** before the suffix maintains the hard pronunciation. For instance, without the hardening effect of the **k**, the word **mimic** would be spelled **mimicing**, with the hard **c** (as in **car**) changing to a soft **c** (as in **notice**). These are words to which this rule applies:

colic	coli**cky**
frolic	froli**cked**, froli**cking**
panic	pani**cky**, pani**cked**, pani**cking**
traffic	traffi**cker**, traffi**cked**, traffi**cking**
picnic	picni**cker**, picni**cked**, picni**cking**

Chapter Mastery Test

Review the spelling rules you have learned in this chapter covering final consonants. Then complete the following questions to test your mastery of these spelling skills.

Part I: In each of the following groups of words, circle the *one* word in which the final consonant does *not* change when **-ed** or **-ing** is added.

1.	extol	adapt	gun
2.	pretend	fib	annul
3.	scrub	disown	control
4.	creak	quiz	swab
5.	stoop	photoset	panic
6.	allot	tempt	format
7.	whir	bar	offend
8.	murmur	flap	inter
9.	expel	accustom	glut
10.	stiff	hum	regret

Part II: In the space provided, correctly spell the words formed from the following root words and suffixes.

1.	plain	+ ness	= _____
2.	planet	+ ary	= _____
3.	god	+ ess	= _____

4. acquit   + al   = _____
5. equal   + ly   = _____
6. inhabit   + able = _____
7. confer   + ence = _____
8. garlic   + y   = _____
9. youthful + ly   = _____
10. trim   + ness = _____

Part III: Circle the correctly spelled choice in each of these sentences.

1. The decaying castle looked [forbiding] [forbidding].
2. This [writing] [writting] assignment is taking longer than I thought.
3. For my father, going on vacation was an unusual [occurence] [occurrence].
4. The fog [enveloped] [envelopped] the town in gray silence.
5. The clown [mimiked] [mimicked] every move Jerome made.
6. She is quite attractive, despite her [manish] [mannish] appearance.
7. Kim was [boiling] [boilling] mad by the time she got home.
8. That answer is only [partially] [partialy] true.
9. She [counselled] [counseled] Joe to wait until next year.
10. Mr. Andrews [regreted] [regretted] his decision to fire Oscar.

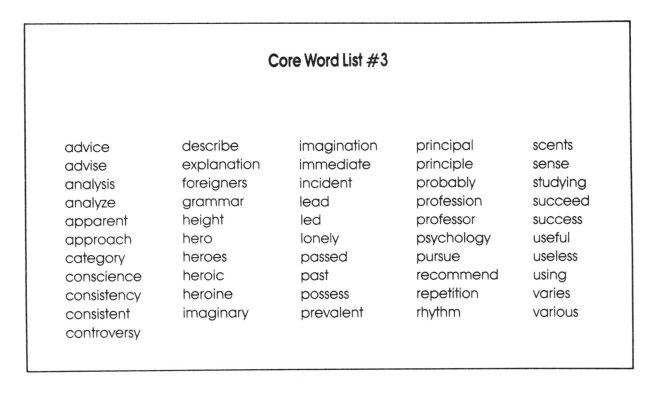

Core Word List #3

advice	describe	imagination	principal	scents
advise	explanation	immediate	principle	sense
analysis	foreigners	incident	probably	studying
analyze	grammar	lead	profession	succeed
apparent	height	led	professor	success
approach	hero	lonely	psychology	useful
category	heroes	passed	pursue	useless
conscience	heroic	past	recommend	using
consistency	heroine	possess	repetition	varies
consistent	imaginary	prevalent	rhythm	various
controversy				

Core Word Mastery Test

Master the spelling of these words from the core list and learn their meanings before you try to learn those in the chapters ahead. **Remember:** *In spelling, your goal is a perfect score.*

Part I: Two words in each of the following sentences have a blank space for *one* letter. Add the appropriate letter.

1. How would you d____scribe your profes____ion?
2. His refusal to answer will prob____bly start a contr____versy.
3. The latest border inc____dent between these nations is merely a rep____tition of what has passed between them many times before.
4. If you choose the cat____gory of eating, you will certainly suc____eed in answering all questions.
5. Have you tried u____ing psyc____ology to influence your children?

Part II: Proofread the following paragraph, correcting all spelling errors.

The lonly proffessor tried without sucess to search his conscience for an explaination of his feeling that he was usless. But no imediate answer was forthcoming. No useful guide led him to truth; no friend could reccoment a potion that might posess special powers to help him.

Part III: Circle the correct word choices in each of the following sentences. Note that although all the choices are correctly spelled in some sentences, only *one* choice is appropriate in context.

1. I have been [lead] [led] by the nose till my feet feel like [lead] [led].
2. What has [passed] [past] between them is now [passed] [past].
3. When I sought his [advice] [advise], he refused to [advice] [advise] me.
4. There is no [scents] [sense] in acting like a child simply because you find that a man of [principal] [principle] cannot attain a [principle] [principal] role in life.
5. If a child [various] [varies] his habits frequently, his parents may have to try [various] [varies] techniques to stabilize their offspring.

Part IV: In the space provided, write the correctly spelled choice for each sentence.

1. Attorneys seek an _____ flaw in their opponent's argument and then expose it.
   (apparant, apparent, apperant)
2. Butlers _____ guests with extraordinary courtesy.
   (approch, approach, aproach)
3. Cooks who create exotic new dishes become _____ in the eyes of their employers.
   (heros, heroez, heroes)
4. Dentists have the mistaken notion that all pain is _____.
   (immaginery, imaginery, imaginary)
5. Electricians need a vocabulary filled with words given them by _____.
   ampere, volt, watt, ohm, and the like.
   (furriners, foreigners, foriegners)

6. Florists _____ weddings and funerals.
   (persue, pursue, purrsue)
7. Geriatrists practice a form of medicine that seeks to deny the _____ notion that the old have outworn their usefulness.
   (prevalent, prevelent, prevelant)
8. Horticulturists _____ crops to determine the best ways to develop new strains of plants, fruits, and vegetables.
   (analyse, analize, analyze)
9. Icemen have been less _____ in arriving on time since the refrigerator became popular.
   (consistant, consisttent, consistent)
10. Janitors often spend hours in the basement quietly listening to the _____ of the oil burner.
    (rythm, rhythmn, rhythm)
11. _____ qualities are attained by those who consistently value principle and will.
    (Herroic, Herioc, Heroic)
12. The beautiful girl had achieved Amazonian _____ but minuscule literacy.
    (height, hieght, heighth)
13. His attempts at _____ always fail because he starts at midnight.
    (studdying, studying, studing)
14. Is it my _____ or has your nose grown?
    (immagination, imagenation, imagination)
15. The _____ of this novel is actually a man in disguise.
    (herroin, heroine, herione)

CHAPTER FOUR

Plurals and Tenses

An Overview: The Parts of Speech

The term "part of speech" refers to the job that a word does in a sentence—its function or use. In English there are eight word functions—in other words, eight parts of speech:

noun, pronoun, verb, adjective, adverb, preposition, conjunction, and interjection. Look over the following chart to familiarize yourself with the different parts of speech:

Part of Speech	Function	Examples
Noun	To name a person, place, thing, quality, state, or action	Adam, Washington, pen, wit, laughter, heat
Pronoun	To substitute for a noun	he, she, it
Verb	To express action or non-action (a state of being)	run, talk, think, is, has, was, will be
Adjective	To modify (describe or limit) a noun or pronoun	*strong* man, *ugly* city, *few* hours, *small* one
Adverb	To modify a verb, adjective, or adverb	think *quickly*, *very* quickly, *unusually* ugly
Preposition	To show the relationship between a noun or pronoun and some other word	cart *before* horse, room *with* a view, somewhere *over* the rainbow
Conjunction	To join two words or two groups of words	Jack *and* Jill, here today *but* gone tomorrow
Interjection	To display emotion	Oh! Gosh! Hurrah!

A word is a noun, verb, adjective, or other part of speech *depending on its use—and on its use only*. In other words, a word is a noun if it is *used* like a **noun—if it names**. It is a preposition if it is *used* like a **preposition— if it shows the relationship between nouns**. For example, study the following passage. Notice how many different ways the word **round** is used:

Our **round** world [**adjective**, modifying the noun **world**]—which I shall **round** [**verb**, expressing action] once more before I die—spins **round** and **round** [**adverb**, modifying the verb **spins**] on its axis, at the same time making a circle **round** the sun [**preposition**, showing relationship between the two nouns, **circle** and **sun**] that results in the **round** of the seasons [**noun**, naming something].

Some words change from one part of speech to another—from a verb to a noun, from a noun to an adjective, from an adjective to an adverb, and so forth—when a suffix is added to or removed from the root word. The spelling rules covering these situations are covered in **Part Three: Putting the Parts Together**. In this chapter, we're going to focus exclusively on how to spell nouns and verbs.

Plural Nouns

One of the chief difficulties in spelling nouns occurs when shifting from the singular to the plural. Learning the following rules will help you overcome this difficulty.

Rule 1: Most nouns add -**s** to become plural. Here are a few examples:

Singular	Plural
boy	boys
home	homes
Greek	Greeks
fraction	fractions
toggle	toggles
rose	roses

Rule 2: Nouns ending in **s**, **ss**, **sh**, **ch**, **x**, and **z** add -**es** to become plural. Look at these examples:

Singular	Plural
glass	glasses
kiss	kisses
crash	crashes
fish	fishes
watch	watches
lunch	lunches
tax	taxes
buzz	buzzes

Check your understanding of the first two rules covering plurals by completing this exercise.

Exercise 4.1

In the space provided, write the plural forms of the following nouns.

1. punch _____
2. house _____
3. ribbon _____
4. paradox _____
5. giggle _____
6. albatross _____
7. consumer _____

8. gazette   _____
9. infant   _____
10. parish   _____

The first two spelling rules covering plural nouns deal with *regular* plurals. However, English has a number of nouns that are *irregular*—that is, they follow odd patterns when changing from singular to plural. The following rules will help you spell irregular plurals correctly.

Rule 3: Some nouns ending in **o** add **-s** to become plural. Others add **-es** to become plural. The only standard guideline you can follow covers nouns ending in **o** preceded by a *vowel*. In such cases, you add **-s**. Here are some examples:

Singular	Plural
radio	radios
patio	patios
rodeo	rodeos
tattoo	tattoos

For nouns ending in **o** preceded by a *consonant* you must simply memorize which ones use **-s** and which use **-es** to form the plural. Study the examples in these lists:

-S Plurals

Singular	Plural
banjo	banjos
piano	pianos
solo	solos
zero	zeros
lasso	lassos
bronco	broncos

tobacco	tobaccos
dynamo	dynamos

-ES Plurals

Singular	Plural
echo	echoes
hero	heroes
veto	vetoes
innuendo	innuendoes
potato	potatoes
Negro	Negroes
mosquito	mosquitoes
cargo	cargoes
domino	dominoes
tornado	tornadoes

Rule 4: Some nouns ending in **f** or **fe** change **f** to **v** and add **-es** to become plural. Other nouns retain the **f** (or the **gh** which makes the **f** sound) and simply add **-s** to become plural. As with nouns ending in **o**, no hard-and-fast principle will guide your spelling of nouns ending in **f** or **fe**. However, you can use certain patterns of pronunciation and spelling to help you memorize which nouns change **f** to **v** to become plural and which do not. Here are some words that illustrate spelling patterns in which the **f** does not change to **v**.

Singular	Plural
belief	beliefs
proof	proofs
surf	surfs
dwarf	dwarfs
puff	puffs
trough	troughs

These are the spelling patterns those words demonstrate:

- nouns with **ie** spelling
- nouns with **oo** spelling
- nouns with **rf** spelling
- nouns with **ff** spelling
- nouns with **gh** spelling

These patterns are *generally* true—which means they don't *always* apply. For instance, **thief** is a noun with **ie** spelling, but the plural is spelled **thieves** (it follows a different rule that will be explained later). Some nouns with **rf** spelling are also exceptions: The plural of **scarf** can be spelled either **scarfs** or **scarves**. The same is true for the plural of **wharf**—either **wharfs** or **wharves**.

Now look at this list of nouns that change the **f** or **fe** to **v** and add **-es** to become plural. Can you pick out pronunciation patterns that will help you know how to spell these words?

Singular	Plural
thief	thie**ves**
leaf	lea**ves**
knife	kni**ves**
life	li**ves**
elf	el**ves**
shelf	shel**ves**

Here are the pronunciation patterns evident in this list:

- nouns pronounced with long **e** (as in **bee**)
- nouns pronounced with long **i** (as in **pie**)
- nouns pronounced with **el** sound (as in **fell**)

Of course, these patterns don't cover every case. For instance, **calf** become **calves** and **loaf** becomes **loaves**. However, you can use these patterns to help you figure out the correct spelling of most plurals of words ending in **f** and **fe**.

Test your grasp of these spelling rules for plurals by doing this exercise.

Exercise 4.2

In the space provided, write the plural forms of the following nouns.

1. studio   _____
2. embargo   _____
3. hoof   _____
4. alto   _____
5. cameo   _____
6. tomato   _____
7. brief   _____
8. wife   _____
9. volcano   _____
10. torso   _____

The next two rules covering plural nouns address words that simply don't follow the usual rules for modern English—nouns that still follow archaic plural forms used in Old English and nouns that are imported into English from other languages.

Rule 5: Most Old English nouns become plural by adding **-en/-ren** or by substituting letters. Some use the same spelling for both singular and plural. Here are examples of all three types:

Add -EN/-REN

Singular	Plural
ox	ox**en**
child	child**ren**
brother	breth**ren**

Substitute Letters

Singular	Plural
foot	f**ee**t
goose	g**ee**se
mouse	m**i**ce
man	m**e**n

No Change

Singular	Plural
deer	deer
sheep	sheep

Not all nouns with the same spelling for both singular and plural forms come from Old English. Here's a list of other words that have the same spelling, no matter how many you are referring to.

barracks	headquarters
clothes	goods
cattle	measles
scissors	pants
species	trousers

Rule 6: Foreign nouns usually follow the rules of their original language when becoming plural in English. English has been enriched by many words from other languages. Most of these words are Latin or Greek, although a number of Spanish, French, and Italian words have also been absorbed into the common vocabulary. In this section we'll just give a general over-view of how to spell the plurals of Latin and Greek nouns. **Chapter 20: Foreign Words and Phrases** will cover other foreign nouns in more detail.

Latin Nouns

Singular	Plural
alum**nus**	alum**ni**
memora**dum**	memoran**da**
append**ix**	append**ices** (or appendixes)

Greek Nouns

Singular	Plural
analys**is**	analys**es**
criter**ion**	criter**ia**

Do this exercise to test your mastery of these rules about plural nouns.

Exercise 4.3

In the space provided, write the plural forms of the following Old English and foreign nouns.

1. tooth _____
2. parenthesis _____
3. child _____
4. headquarters _____
5. medium _____
6. basis _____
7. louse _____
8. focus _____
9. synopsis _____
10. addendum _____

The last few rules governing plural nouns cover unusual situations—such as when the noun is compound or when it is just a letter or number.

Rule 7: Compound nouns add -**s** (sometimes -**es**) to the **main** word in the compound to become plural. Sometimes the main word comes first in the series; other times it comes last. *You* must determine which word is most important to the meaning of the compound. Here are some examples:

Singular	**Plural**
mother-in-law	mother**s**-in-law
passer-by	passer**s**-by
attorney-at-law	attorney**s**-at-law
notary public	notar**ies** public
brigadier general	brigadier general**s**
schoolbook	schoolbook**s**
teaspoonful	teaspoonful**s**

Rule 8: Proper nouns generally add -**s** to become plural. Proper nouns are the specific names of people, places, or things. For instance, the word **Odessa** is a proper noun. So is **Marilyn**. Here are sentences using plural proper nouns, just to give you an idea of how you might use them.

○ I know of two **Odessas** in the world—one in Texas and one in Russia.
○ There are four **Marilyns** working in my office building.

Rule 9: Letters, numbers, and abbreviations add **apostrophe s ('s)** to become plural. Here are some sample sentences using plural letters, numbers, and abbreviations:

○ Be sure to cross your **t's** and dot your **i's**.

○ Without my glasses, all the **8's** look like **3's**.
○ She has five **Ph.D.'s**, although three are only honorary.

Note: Plurals of nouns ending in **y** have not been included in this chapter, since they were covered in **Chapter 2: Final E and Final Y**.

Before you learn the spelling rules covering **verb tenses**, let's test your skill with these last few rules governing plural nouns.

Exercise 4.4

In the space provided, write the plural forms of the following nouns.

1. commander
   in chief   _____
2. Justin   _____
3. handful   _____
4. P   _____
5. Washington   _____
6. lieutenant
   colonel   _____
7. 5   _____
8. M.D.   _____
9. court-martial   _____
10. classroom   _____

Verb Tenses

Many of the important spelling rules affecting verbs have been covered in other chapters of this book. For instance, **Chapter 2: Final E and Final Y** and **Chapter 3: Final**

Consonants. However, this section addresses the basic rules for regular verbs and provides an extensive list of irregular verbs.

Rule 1: Regular verbs show **past tense form** by adding **-ed**, **-t**, or **-d** to the **present tense form** of the verb. The past tense forms include the **simple past tense** and the **past participle**, which usually follows the word **have**. (For example: **Simple past tense** = "I talked." **Past participle** = "I have talked.") Here are some more examples of Rule 1:

Present	Past	Past Participle
talk	talked	talked
fool	fooled	fooled
deal	dealt	dealt
keep	kept	kept
love	loved	loved
grumble	grumbled	grumbled

Rule 2: Irregular verbs show **past tense form** by changing and adding letters. This can cause serious spelling problems, since the past tense form of the word may seem unrelated to its present tense form! Unfortunately, the only way to master the spelling of these verbs is by memorization. Here is a list of commonly used irregular verbs:

Present	Past	Past Participle
awake	awaked, awoke	awaked
bear	bore	borne
begin	began	begun
bid	bade	bidden
break	broke	broken
burst	burst	burst
dive	dived, dove	dived

drink	drank	drunk
flee	fled	fled
fly	flew	flown
forsake	forsook	forsaken
hang	hung, hanged	hung, hanged
know	knew	known
lay	laid	laid
lie	lay	lain
light	lit, lighted	lit, lighted
ring	rang	rung
rise	rose	risen
sing	sang	sung
slay	slew	slain
slink	slunk	slunk
speak	spoke	spoken
sting	stung	stung
stink	stank, stunk	stunk
swear	swore	sworn
swim	swam	swum
wake	woke, waked	waked
wring	wrung	wrung
write	wrote	written

Rule 3: Verbs add **-s** to become singular; without the added **-s**, they are plural. You can improve both your spelling and grammar if you remember that nouns acting as subjects of sentences must *agree* with the verb in *number*. In other words, if the noun is singular, the verb must be singular as well. On the other hand, if the noun is plural, the verb must be, too. **Verbs** add **-s** to become *singular*, but **nouns** add **-s** to become *plural*. Study these examples:

Singular

The dog	barks.
[singular noun subject]	[singular verb adds **-s**]

Plural

The dogs   bark.
  [plural noun   [plural verb]
  subject adds **-s**]

Do the following exercise to test your ability to correctly spell verbs in different tense forms.

Exercise 4.5

In the spaces provided, write the past tense form and past participle form of the following regular and irregular verbs.

	Past Tense	Past Participle
1. sleep	_____	_____
2. laugh	_____	_____
3. grow	_____	_____
4. delay	_____	_____
5. cost	_____	_____
6. remind	_____	_____
7. worry	_____	_____
8. hide	_____	_____
9. slap	_____	_____
10. think	_____	_____
11. dignify	_____	_____
12. rise	_____	_____
13. cut	_____	_____
14. bribe	_____	_____
15. draw	_____	_____

Chapter Mastery Test

Review the spelling rules you have learned in this chapter covering **plural nouns** and **verb tenses**. Then complete the following questions to test your mastery of these spelling skills.

Part I: Circle the correctly spelled choice in each of these sentences.

1. What caused those bright [flashs] [flashes] in the northern sky?
2. Many nineteenth-century [Negroes] [Negros] made important scientific discoveries.
3. Hand me the [scissor] [scissors], please.
4. The experimental school borrows ideas from the [curricula] [curriculums] of schools all over the country.
5. The recipe calls for three [teaspoonsful] [teaspoonfuls] of sugar.
6. "Better safe than sorry" is one of our favorite [mottoes] [mottos].
7. My aunt has a lovely collection of antique [cameoes] [cameos].
8. Geologists study the [strata] [stratum] of minerals that compose the earth's crust.
9. Our daily lives are filled with so many minor [crisises] [crises] we never seem to get ahead.
10. Of the ten contestants, three were [runner-ups] [runners-up].
11. He has three rose [quartzes] [quartzs] in his rock collection.
12. All the choir members are [altoes] [altos].
13. From the observation deck you can look out over the [roofs] [rooves] of the city.
14. A pack of [wolfs] [wolves] howled outside the cabin door.
15. [Mases] [Masses] of bargain hunters stampeded into the store.
16. My uncle has a small herd of [buffalo] [buffalos] on his ranch.
17. Don't let the children play with [matches] [matchs]!

18. Egotists are quite fond of [themselfs] [themselves].
19. Three [wives] [wifes] seem to be more than any man could handle.
20. The mushroom is only one of many different forms of [fungus] [fungi].

Part II: In the space provided, correct the errors in verb form in the following sentences. **Example:** The skunk stinked.
stank _____

1. His boss fired him because he had **drank** on the job. _____
2. The sun **bursted** through from behind the clouds. _____

3. I could have **swore** I heard a noise outside the window. _____
4. After he **begun** his speech, hecklers started throwing things. _____
5. A bee **stang** me on the nose at the picnic. _____
6. In the game of life you must play the hand that life **dealed** you. _____
7. John had **flew** all the way to Chicago without his wallet. _____
8. I **lay** down my burden and **laid** down to rest. _____
9. He **drownded** in the big flood of '82. _____
10. She **awaked** to the fact that he was no good. _____

Core Word List #4

appear	consider	embarrass	Negro	preferred
appearance	considerably	exercise	Negroes	procedure
approaches	convenience	foreign	operate	proceed
arise	convenient	guidance	opinion	prominent
arising	difference	imagine	opponent	refer
character	different	independence	opportunity	referred
characteristic	disappoint	irrelevant	oppose	referring
characterize	dominant	irresistible	optimism	sense
conceivable	efficiency	irritable	precede	tried
conceive	efficient	maintenance	predominant	tries

Core Word Mastery Test

Master the spelling of these words from the core list and learn their meanings before you try to learn those in the chapters ahead. **Remember:** *In spelling, your goal is a perfect score.*

Part I: Each of the core list words in the following sentences either *needs an additional letter* or *has an extra letter.* In either case, correct the spelling.

1. The boxer's oponent outweighed him by twenty-five pounds.

2. In my oppinion, your taste in hats is absurd.
3. Will you excercise your right to vote at the trustees' meeting?
4. How would you charcterize a man who beats his children but not his horse?
5. I will not disapoint you by being present at your next party.
6. Red-headed girls often make a striking appearrance.
7. We should have prefered that Alfred not leave school before finishing.
8. What proceedure ought I follow in acquiring my visa?
9. I cannot immagine a purple cow, and I have no desire to see one.
10. No real diference separates identical twins.
11. All arguments that disagree with mine I dismiss as irelevant.
12. Frankly, I think your optimissm is misplaced.
13. I should not like to emmbarrass my hostess by leaving too early.
14. Why do promminent financiers exaggerate their incomes to everyone except the tax bureau?
15. Some forreign words are familiar to everybody.

Part II: Proofread the following sentences, correcting all spelling errors.

1. Booker T. Washington achieved heroic stature, not only as a negroe but, more importantly, as a man.
2. She tries to achieve the impossible, which she has tryed many times before, but to no avail.
3. He refuses to reffer to the mass thinking of the mob to develop an oppinoin as to which course he should follow.

4. He concieves that the perdomminant ingredient in Mexican food is hot peppers.
5. Joshua's choreography seems to be arrising from body sensation and proseeding to thoughtless motion.

Part III: In the space provided, write the correct choice for each sentence below.

1. To whom have you _____ your maid?
   (referred, refered, refferred)
2. I think it _____ that oysters appear in June.
   (conceiveable, conceivable, concievable)
3. Which _____ of the mosquito did you list in your notes?
   (charcteristic, charactaristic, characteristic)
4. Correct spelling is a necessity not a _____.
   (convenience, conveneince, conveniance)
5. Typing _____ increases with practice.
   (efficeincy, efficiency, efficiancy)
6. The investors looked at the rising prices as a cause for _____.
   (optimmism, optimism, optimasm)
7. Why do some women get _____ when you tell them the truth?
   (iritable, irritable, irritible)
8. The _____ expenses for a motorboat are high.
   (maintainance, maintenence, maintenance)
9. I have grown _____ older since we last met.

(considerably, consideribly, considerrably)

10. Every modern high school has a _____ department to help young people select an appropriate vocation. (guidence, giudance, guidance)

Part IV: Match the core list word in *Column B* with the appropriate context in *Column A*. If the core list word is misspelled, correct it. **Example:** Where are they eating tonight? (dining, slepping, shooting) *Answer:* dining

Column A
1. I'm against it.
2. Will you get up?
3. They are simply unalike.
4. He works effectively.
5. He has a strong personality.
6. Your chance has come.
7. I find it most handy.
8. I want my freedom.
9. What happened before?
10. Can you describe his personality?

Column B
a. convenient
b. independance
c. preceed
d. diferant
e. efficeincy
f. dominant
g. arrise
h. charcter
i. opose
j. opporttunity

CHAPTER FIVE

Capitalization

Capitalization is the way we indicate certain facts or add certain elements of meaning to words. For instance, some words that are capitalized in one of the following sentences aren't capitalized in the other.

As *Mother* walked down *Main Avenue,* she sipped a *Coca-Cola*.

As my *mother* walked down the *main avenue,* she sipped a *cola*.

What information does capitalizing or not capitalizing give us? If you're not exactly sure of the answer, study the following spelling rules for capitalization. You'll soon have this area of spelling mastered.

Rule 1: Capitalize the first word in a sentence, in a quotation, and in a line of poetry. Consider these examples:

○ **A** man must eat.
○ **Calvin** Coolidge wrote, "**In** a republic the law reflects rather than makes the standard of conduct and the state of popular opinion."
○ **So** long as men can breathe, or eyes can see,
So long lives this, and this gives life to thee. (Shakespeare)

Rule 2: Capitalize proper nouns. There are many different categories of proper nouns. Here are some examples for each category.

○ **Proper names:** Andrew Jackson, California, Europe, Old Blue

○ **Specific place names:** Tobacco Road, Lake Superior, Fifth Avenue, the North Pole, the Midwest, Harvard University

○ **Specific events, historical periods, and holidays:** World War II, Independence Day, the Middle Ages, the Cold War

○ **Specific agreements, laws, etc.:** the Warsaw Pact, the Sherman Antitrust Law, the First Amendment

○ **Races, ethnic groups, languages, and religions:** Caucasian, Negro, Spanish, Arabic, Jewish, Protestant, Buddhism

○ **Companies, organizations, and clubs:** General Motors Corporation, Associated Press, Chamber of Commerce, Veterans of Foreign Wars, the Democratic Party

○ **Official bodies:** the United States Senate, the Florida Legislature, the Supreme Court

○ **Titles of people, used with proper names, heads of state, heads of church, Cabinet officers:** the President of the United States, the Pope, the Prime Minister, the Dalai Lama, Queen Elizabeth, Colonel Williams, Mrs. Jones, the Secretary of State

○ **References to the Deity and sacred works:** God, Jehovah, Brahma, Christ, His word, the Bible, the Koran

○ **Personifications and nicknames:** Death (as in "Death, where is thy sting"), Love (as in "I am become a slave to Love"), Little China, the Big Apple, the Big Bopper

○ **Trade names:** Coke, Xerox, Chanel No. 5, Ivory soap

○ **Days, months:** Monday, October

Rule 3: Capitalize words that signify family relationships when used as a title or as a substitute for a proper name. Here are some examples:

Title:
○ He's bringing Aunt Dorothy with him.
○ I call my stepfather Papa Jim.

Substitute name:
○ We haven't seen Granny for a year.
○ If I ask Father, I know he'll say yes.
○ Mom, will you take me to the store?

Note: When the word signifying family relationship is preceded by a possessive, *don't* capitalize. For example:

○ My aunt Dorothy is coming with him.
○ I asked my mom to take me to the store.

Rule 4: Capitalize the titles of published or produced works. However, don't capitalize every word—just be sure to capitalize the first and last words and all the *main* words in between. In general, you need not capitalize articles (**the, a, an**), conjunctions (**and, but, or, nor**), and prepositions (**to, for, of, from**). Here are examples of the various kinds of written works:

○ **Books:** *To Kill a Mockingbird*
○ **Magazines:** *U.S. News and World Report*
○ **Newspapers:** *The Washington Post*
○ **Plays:** *The Fantasticks*
○ **Movies:** *Romancing the Stone*
○ **Stories:** "A Rose for Emily"
○ **Articles:** "How to Update Your Kitchen"
○ **Songs:** "America the Beautiful"

When Not to Capitalize

Because the rules for capitalization can be tricky, here are some guidelines to help you remember when **not** to capitalize.

○ **Don't capitalize** nonspecific names of places or events:
   Students at the **university** protested the new ruling.
   Thousands of soldiers died in the last **war**.
○ **Don't capitalize** most nonspecific titles —those not combined with a proper name:

Every boy wants to be **president** (refers to the office, not a specific person).
The **senator** will be arriving soon.
The **colonel** reprimanded the **sergeant**.
The **doctor** said Jeff would be well in a week.
○ **Don't capitalize** directions:
   We headed **north** up the coast highway.
   The best view from his house is toward the **southwest**.
○ **Don't capitalize** the seasons:
   Last **winter** a blizzard struck the entire region.
   We have a reunion every **spring**.

Chapter Mastery Test

Review the spelling rules you have learned in this chapter covering **capitalization**. Then complete the following questions to test your mastery of these spelling skills.

Part I: In the space provided, rewrite the following passages, capitalizing all the words that require an initial capital letter.

1. the city of nome, alaska, acquired its name through error. there was a small prospectors' settlement known as anvil city on the seward peninsula in alaska. a washington clerk drawing a map did not know its name and wrote "name?" at that place on the map. one of his superiors took the word for "nome" and that name still stands.

_____

_____

_____

_____

_____

_____

2. *myths for the modern*, edited by philip corey and william rogers, was published by avon books. perhaps the best story in it is "odysseus of the 80's," by mark schultz. in this adaptation of homeric legend, a modern odysseus drives a cadillac and drinks perrier. unlike his greek namesake, this hero is no hero at all—just a yuppie trying to win the rat race.

---

3. what is africa to me:
   copper sun or scarlet sea,
   jungle star or jungle track,
   strong bronzed men, or regal black
   women from whose loins i sprang
   when the birds of eden sang? (from "heritage" by countee cullen)

---

4. it is the grace of god that urges missionaries to suffer the most disheartening privations for the faith. this grace moved st. isaac jogues to say (when he came to canada), "i felt as if it were a christmas day for me, and that i was to be born again to a new life, to a life in him."

---

5. when the south seceded from the united states—and thereby sparked the civil war—the leaders of the confederacy could not have known the devastation that the conflict would cause both sides. more american lives were lost in the war between the states than in both world war I and world war II combined. after general lee surrendered at appomattox, the stars and stripes flew once again over a union of states, but the division of spirits lasted until the turn of the century.

Core Word List #5

aggressive	humor	original	satire	suppress
amicable	humorist	philosophy	satirize	technique
arguing	humorous	prefer	seize	temperament
argument	hypocrisy	propaganda	seizure	therefore
auxiliary	hypocrite	propagate	sergeant	together
control	independent	psychoanalysis	sophomore	tragedy
controlled	inveigh	psychopathic	subtle	tyranny
fulfill	inveigle	resonant	summary	unusual
further	irresistible	ridicule	summed	unusually
hindrance	origin	ridiculous	suppose	villain

Core Word Mastery Test

Master the spelling of these words from the core list and learn their meanings before you try to learn those in the chapters ahead. **Remember:** *In spelling, your goal is a perfect score.*

Part I: Match the core list word in *Column B* with the appropriate context in *Column A*. If the core list word is misspelled, correct it.

Column A
1. The unfortunate man is mad.
2. The doctor uses Freud's methods.
3. He has an amusing cast of mind.
4. The hero dies at the end.
5. He pretends to be what he is not.
6. His reasoning is deft and ingenious.
7. What sort of disposition has he?
8. He is a despicable fellow.
9. That concise statement gives me the general idea.
10. The student is starting her second year at school.

Column B
a. humor
b. hyppocrite
c. temprament
d. villian
e. sophmore
f. psycopathic
g. phycoanalysis
h. suptle
i. tradgedy
j. summery

Part II: In the space provided, write the correct choice for each sentence below.

1. A cogent _____ is always persuasive.
   (arguement, argument, arrgument)
2. Dress designers forever seek fresh, _____ patterns.
   (orriginel, originel, original)
3. I have never found slapstick particularly _____.
   (humerous, humorous, humorus)
4. _____ is an homage Vice pays to Virtue.
   (Hypocracy, Hyprocisy, Hypocrisy)
5. On what groundwork of knowledge have you built your _____?
   (philosophy, pholosophy, filosophy)
6. In the kitchen most husbands are more _____ than help.
   (hinderance, hindrence, hindrance)
7. Why do you mock and _____ that poor but honest fool?
   (redicule, ridecule, ridicule)
8. _____ exposes man's foibles and laughs at them.
   (Sattire, Satire, Satyre)
9. Your acute observation _____ up my feelings precisely.
   (summed, sumed, sunned)
10. Tyrants attempt to _____ popular expressions of opinion.
    (surpress, suppress, supress)

Part III: One of the core list words in each of the following sentences needs an *additional* letter to make it correct. Add the necessary letter.

1. I have controled my temper too long.
2. Down with tyrany! Long live democracy!

3. A peaceful man restrains his agressive tendencies.
4. Supose then that I were in your place.
5. What an unusal way to eat peas—with a straw.
6. New techiques for increasing reading speed are now available for all.
7. What is needed therefor is a good five-cent candy bar.
8. Usually he is late, but tonight he is unusualy so.
9. Someday we may have a television humrist who is truly comic.
10. Why do Army privates always have such strong feelings about their sergants?

Part IV: Proofread the following sentences, correcting all spelling errors.

1. Further argueing about how their government propegates properganda seems rediculous.
2. We must work toggether to expose the orrigin of such thinking and, finally, to satirise the men who foist it upon the people.
3. An indededependent man preferrs to consider his own thinking as valid.
4. His charms I find iresistible; however, his friends are less than ammicable.
5. We cannot inviegh against such unfairness too strongly, nor can we sieeze the reins of power too firmly.
6. He invihgled granny out of her life savings with his flashing blue eyes and rezonent baritone voice.
7. Following the spy's sezure by the German captain, the remaining members of the underground implemented the auxillary plan.

PART TWO

SNEAKING UP ON SNEAKY SPELLINGS

CHAPTER SIX

Lost-and-Found Sounds

This chapter and the other chapters in this section address the special problems you face when trying to spell according to pronunciation. **Chapter 7: Silent Letters** and **Chapter 8: Sound-Alike Words** cover inconsistencies in the language itself—identical letter combinations that sound very different in different words or identical sounds that are written using very different letter combinations. Quite often, the only way to master the spelling of these words is through memorization.

However, a large number of words are commonly *misspelled* because they are commonly *mispronounced*. Sounds that belong *in* are left *out*—or sounds that *shouldn't* be there are put *in*! This chapter looks at these kinds of "sound" misspellings.

To master "sound" spelling, you must follow these steps:

1. **Say the word slowly to yourself before you write it.** Break the word into syllables and carefully pronounce each syllable.
2. **Say the word again—syllable by syllable—as you write it.**
3. **Say the word one last time as you read it.**

Remember, you can improve your spelling by paying careful attention to your pronunciation.

Lost Sounds

Sounds get "lost" when we "swallow" or "drop" them as we speak the word. As with most languages, spoken English is less formal than written English—both in pronunciation and in grammar. Unless we are delivering a speech or talking to someone important, we don't worry too much about enunciating each word clearly. However, our spelling will always suffer if we don't remember that those "lost" sounds are there. Study the following examples of vowel sounds that frequently get "lost":

Lost Vowel Sounds

	Correct	**Incorrect**
a	boundary [BOWN-da-ree]	boundry [BOWN-dree]
	temperament [TEM-pur-a-mint]	temperment [TEM-pur-mint]
	separate [SEP-a-ret]	seprate [SEP-ret]
e	every [EV-ur-ee]	evry [EV-ree]
	interested [IN-tur-est-ed]	intrested [IN-trest-ed]
	mathematics [MATH-e-mat-iks]	mathmatics [MATH-mat-iks]
i	business [BIZ-i-ness]	busness [BIZ-ness]
	quiet [KWY-et]	quite [KWYT]
	auxiliary [awks-IL-ya-ree]	auxillary [awks-IL-a-ree]
o	chocolate [CHOK-a-let]	choclate [CHOK-let]
	sophomore [SAWF-u-mawr]	sophmore [SAWF-mawr]
	favorite [FAY-vu-rit]	favrite [FAYV-rit]
u	conspicuous [kun-SPIK-yew-us]	conspicuos [kun-SPIK-yus]
	strenuous [STREN-yew-us]	strenuos [STREN-yus]

In some words the vowels in unaccented syllables are hard to hear, even when the word is pronounced correctly. Even though the sound isn't "lost," it might be difficult to recognize. For example, say the word **rel-ative** (*rel-a-tive*). Just hearing the word, you might not be able to tell whether the middle syllable is an **i** (*relitive*), an **e** (*reletive*), or an **a** (*relative*). The weak vowel sound is "over-powered" by the strongly accented syllable that comes before it.

How can you overcome the spelling problem caused by weak vowels? Think of another word in the same word family. For instance, if you cannot remember how to spell **relative**, think of the root word **relate**. Or for a word like **politics**, with a weak vowel **i**, think of the word **political**. In these cases, the vowel sounds are strong and easy to identify. Look over these examples:

To spell. . .	**Think of. . .**
humorous	hum*or*
college	coll*e*giate
pacify	Pa*ci*fic
medicine	me*di*cinal
hypocrisy	hypo*cri*tical

Consonant sounds can also be misplaced, causing us to misspell words. Check out this list of commonly "lost" *consonant* sounds:

Lost Consonant Sounds

	Correct	Incorrect
c	arctic [ARK-tik]	artic [AR-tik]
	succinct [suk-SINGT]	sussinct [sus-SINGT]
d	thousand [THOW-zand]	thousan [THOW-zan]
	candidate [CAN-du-dayt]	canidate [CAN-u-dayt]
g	recognize [REK-og-nyz]	reconize [REK-uh-nyz]
	strength [STRENKTH]	strenth [STRENTH]
l	all right [AWL RYT]	awright [AW RYT]
n	government [GUV-urn-mint]	goverment [GUV-ur-mint]
r	library [LY-bra-ree]	libary [LY-ba-ree]
t	exactly [eg-ZAKT-lee]	exackly [eg-ZAK-lee]
	district [DIS-trikt]	distric [DIS-trik]

Before you go on to learn about other spelling errors caused by mispronunciation, do this exercise to test your ability to correctly spell words with "lost" vowel and consonant sounds.

Exercise 6.1

Circle the correctly spelled choice in each of the following sentences. Be sure to carefully pronounce each choice before selecting the one you believe is correct.

1. Joshua brought her a bouquet of sweet purple [vilets] [violets].
2. Her hands, arms, and neck flashed with the sparkle of hundreds of [jewels] [jewls].
3. We think of the Smiths more as [acquaintances] [aquaintances] than as close friends.
4. When his mother tells him to clean his room, Johnny usually says ["Aw right"] ["All right"] and then forgets all about it.
5. [Incidently] [Incidentally], I won't be able to meet you for dinner.
6. In emergencies people often suddenly find they have the [strenth] [strength] to lift very heavy objects.
7. She enjoyed the rare [privlege] [privilege] of a night of complete privacy.
8. Which congressional [district] [districk] do you live in?
9. Check out a person's [background] [backround] before hiring him to do an important job.
10. My grandparents slept in [seprate] [separate] bedrooms for as long as I can remember.

Found Sounds

A certain group of words are frequently misspelled because of a different problem with pronunciation—adding sounds that don't belong or scrambling sounds so they are in the wrong order. Study the following lists of words and note the correct pronunciation for each.

Correct	Incorrect
across [a-KROS]	acrost [a-KROST]
athletic [ATH-le-tik]	atheletic [ATH-a-le-tik]
attack [a-TAK]	attackt [a-TAKT]
attacked [a-TAKT]	attackted [a-TAK-ted]
column [KOL-um]	coliumn [KOL-yum]
drowned [DROWND]	drownded [DROWND-ed]
escape [es-KAYP]	excape [egz-KAYP]
grievous [GREEV-us]	grievious [GREEV-ee-us]
height [HYT]	heighth [HYT'TH]
mischievous [MIS-tchiv-us]	mischevious [mis-TCHEEV-ee-us]
once [WUNS]	onct [WUNST]

Notice that these words reveal several patterns of misspelling based upon mispronunciation. Try to be aware of adding these unnecessary "found" sounds:

- -t following an s sound
- -t following a k sound
- -ed following a d sound
- -i- before the letters -ous
- -y- before the letter -u

Sometimes words are misspelled because they are pronounced with the sounds out-of-place. The following words are commonly misspelled for this reason:

Correct	Incorrect
children [CHIL-dren]	childern [CHIL-dern]
irrelevant [ir-REL-u-vant]	irrevelant [ir-REV-u-lant]
hundred [HUN-dred]	hunderd [HUN-derd]
perspiration [pur-spu-RAY-shun]	prespiration [pres-pu-RAY-shun]
larynx [LAR-inks]	larnyx [LAHR-niks]
cavalry [KAV-ul-ree]	calvary [KAL-vu-ree]
incongruous [in-KON-grew-us]	incongerous [in-KON-ger-us]
jewelry [JEW-el-ree]	jewelry [JEWL-er-ee]

Before you attempt the chapter mastery test, do the following exercise on "found" and misplaced sounds.

Exercise 6.2

Circle the correctly spelled choice in the following sentences. Be sure to carefully pronounce each choice before selecting the one you believe is correct.

1. I agree with you, but my [partener] [partner] may not.
2. Frank's comments all seemed [irrevelant] [irrelevant] to the subject we were discussing.

3. He had developed an elaborate [excape] [escape] plan that seemed foolproof.
4. Stephanie wanted to sit [besides] [beside] her mother at dinner.
5. The dress [pattren] [pattern] was several sizes too large for Beth.
6. Just when everything looked impossible, the [cavalry] [calvary] came riding in.
7. The repairman came to fix the [warshing] [washing] machine today.
8. Judith and Claire wore [exsactly] [exactly] the same costume to the Halloween party.
9. Every thirteen-year-old girl should have a [dairy] [diary] to tell her secrets to.
10. Those children are terribly [mischievous] [mischevious] at school.

Chapter Mastery Test

Review the spelling rules you have learned in this chapter covering **lost-and-found sounds**. Then complete the following questions to test your mastery of these spelling skills.

Part I: Circle or underline the *one* correctly spelled word in each of these word groups. Be sure to carefully pronounce each choice before selecting the one you believe is correct.

1. strickly	strictly	stricly
2. governor	govenor	governer
3. suprize	surprise	supprise
4. accidently	accidentaly	accidentally
5. intrest	interest	intarest
6. miniature	miniture	minature
7. hundered	hunderd	hundred
8. prevail	pervail	praveil
9. crool	crule	cruel
10. complimentry	complimentory	complimentary
11. Febuary	Febrary	February
12. hindrance	hinderance	hindrence
13. persprire	prespire	perspire
14. mathematic	mathmatic	mathamatic
15. disastrous	disasterous	disastarous

Part II: Provide the missing vowel for each word in the following pairs.

1. acad_____my   acad_____mic
2. compet_____tive   compet_____tion
3. myst_____ry   myst_____rious
4. r_____dicule   r_____diculous
5. ap_____logy   ap_____logetic
6. friv_____lous   friv_____lity

7. coll_____ge   coll_____giate
8. ben_____fit   ben_____ficial
9. pol_____tics   pol_____tical
10. med_____cine   med_____cinal
11. hypocr_____sy   hypocr_____te
12. d_____spair   d_____sprate
13. defin_____te   defin_____tion
14. temp_____rate   temp_____rature
15. gramm_____r   gramm_____tical

Core Word List #6

academic	accidental	capitol	disciple	fundamental
academically	accidentally	challenge	discipline	fundamentally
academy	across	Christ	doesn't	length
accept	article	Christian	etc.	lengthening
acceptable	basically	Christianity	exceed	outrageous
acceptance	basis	coming	excess	salable
accepting	blamable	curiosity	excessive	speaking
access	Britain	curious	familiar	strength
accessible	Britannica	decided	finally	you're
accident	capital	decision	frivolous	

Core Word Mastery Test

Master the spelling of these words from the core list and learn their meanings before you try to learn those in the chapters ahead.

Remember: *In spelling, your goal is a perfect score.*

Part I: Write the appropriate suffix in the space to complete the core list word.

1. Academic_____ (-ly, -aly, -ally) speaking, he is not doing very good work.
2. The roadway has been repaired and is now access_____ (-able, -ible).
3. The nominee made his accept_____ (-ence, -ance) speech before a happy audience.

4. The boy's request for an increase in allowance was accept_____ (-ible, -able) to his parents.
5. Is the presence of a fly in my soup really accident_____ (-al, -el)?
6. Did the soldier shoot himself in the foot accident_____ (-ly, -elly, -ally) or purposely?
7. I am basic_____ (-ly, -ally, -illy) in accord with your views.
8. We have final_____ (-y, -ly) arrived at our point of embarkation.
9. There can be no fundament_____ (-il, -al, -el) distinction between identical twins.
10. Although details need to be clarified, his essay is fundament_____ (-ly, -ally, -elly) sound.

Part II: Circle the *one* correct word choice in each of the following sentences.

1. After much deliberation the jury reached a [descision] [decision].
2. Many great writers belong to the American [Accademy] [Academy] of Arts and Letters.
3. I have been granted [axcess] [access] to the department's secret files.
4. The dominant religion in Western Europe is [Cristianity] [Christianity].
5. The *Encyclopaedia [Brittanica] [Britannica]* is one of the most important reference books in the world.
6. The automobile [accident] [aciddent] cost two men their lives.
7. Look [across] [accross] the field.
8. Her attention to detail is [eccessive] [excessive] to the point of madness.

9. She has a searching and relentless [curosity] [curiosity] about the nature of things.
10. A wayward child needs gentle but firm [dissipline] [discipline].
11. Estelle always shows up at parties with an [outragous] [outrageous] hairdo.
12. In Washington we first visited the [Capitol][Capitel] building.
13. We ended up with an [eccess] [excess] of peanut butter and no jelly.
14. I shall [challenge] [challange] him to a duel.
15. Don't turn your back when I am [speeking] [speaking] to you!

Part III: One of the core list words in each of the following sentences contains an *extra* letter that causes a misspelling. Remove the extra letter.

1. I remember when Brittain really ruled the waves.
2. The quarterback's acaddemic record was not spectacularly good.
3. Androclus was a Roman by birth, a Christtian by faith.
4. Lenghthening or shortening hemlines seems to be the major activity of the contemporary fashion designer.
5. I can find no logical bassis for lowering standards for admission to college.
6. Whom did you meet while comming through the rye?
7. Familliar faces need not always be welcome sights.
8. I am curious to learn how one so dull became so successful.
9. Every leader has a band of discipeles who follow him slavishly.

10. I acceppt your terms unconditionally.
11. Despite the hurricane damage, I still believe this house is sallable.
12. If Lydia weren't so frivvolous, she could have had a brilliant career.
13. Of course he is blamabble, but does blaming help resolve the situation?
14. Although she was bold, Miss Marple never would exxceed the limits of propriety.
15. My dad used to say, "Invest all your cappital in real estate."

Part IV: Proofread the following passage, correcting all errors in spelling.

I have decidid that your artecle does'nt have enough strenth of conviction. Before acepting it, I should like you to increase its lenkth, strenthen its style, and support its arguments more forcefully. When, for example, your'e speeking of Chrisst, Buddha, Lao-Tse, ect., you need to draw clearer distinctions among them.

CHAPTER SEVEN

Silent Letters

In some languages words are spelled exactly as they sound—each letter or letter combination has a particular sound all its own. But English obviously isn't one of those languages!

For more than two hundred years, well-educated and well-intentioned people have tried to establish a logical connection between the sound (phonetics) and the spelling of English words. Unfortunately, they have had only limited success. As a result, we are stuck with inconsistencies between words that make proper pronunciation and correct spelling a big challenge. Here are the two main problem areas:

Problem 1: Pronunciation may change while spelling stays the same. Look at these examples:

ea   lead [LEED] — verb meaning to go in advance

lead [LED] — noun naming a heavy metal

tear [TAYR] — verb meaning to pull apart

tear [TEER] — noun naming a drop of liquid from the eye

ough   though [thOH]

through [THREW]

cough [KOF]

hicc**ough** [HIK-up]
t**ough** [TUF]
dr**ough**t [DROWT]

Problem 2: Spelling may change while pronunciation stays the same. Here are some examples of this problem:

OO	moon	**K**	spike
	fruit		lick
	sue		antique
	group		biscuit
	rude		account
	maneuver		acquaint
	flew		frolic
AY	aide	**SH**	ocean
	payment		chandelier
	suede		special
	break		sugar
	veil		conscience
	obey		tissue
	neighbor		nation

With this much complexity, figuring out which of the many different letters and letter combinations to use when spelling a certain sound is like solving a giant puzzle. Adding to the complexity are the many "silent" letters used in English words—letters that represent no sound at all! This chapter is designed to help you master "soundless" spelling.

Silent Vowels

The silent **e** is a well-known character in English. In many instances, the silent **e** signals that the *single* vowel in the preceding syllable should be pronounced with a "long" sound—like the long **a** in **cake**, the long **e** in **compete**, the long **i** in **recite**, the long **o** in **scope**, or the long **u** in **fuse**. However, that's not always the case, especially in multi-syllable words like **climate**, **expletive**, and **nicotine**. The silent **e** is also used to soften the **c** sound at the end of words like **practice**, **novice**, and **efface**—otherwise, it would carry the **k** sound of **frolic** or **mimic**. Most people don't have too much trouble remembering to include the silent **e** when spelling common words.

Most "silent" vowels, however, aren't actually *silent*—they are paired with other vowels to form a *digraph* (two letters used to represent a single sound)—**ai** as in **pair**, **ea** as in **threat**, **ei** as in **receipt**, **ou** as in **could**, and so forth. For the most part, these spelling challenges are covered in other sections of this book.

Silent Consonants

Certain consonants lose their "voices" when in the vicinity of certain other consonants. They simply don't "speak up." When these pairs of consonants come at the beginning of a word, the first letter is usually silent. For example, the word **gnarled** is pronounced NAWRLD—the **g** is silent. Other examples of the **gn** consonant combination are **gnaw** (pronounced **NAW**) and **gnat** (pronounced **NAT**). Here are other examples of consonant combinations in which the first letter is silent:

kn: know, knife, knight, knot
pn: pneumonia, pneumatic
ps: psychic, psychology, psalm
wr: write, wring, wreck, wreath

Sometimes the second letter is silent, as in these examples:

gh: **gh**ost, **gh**etto, **gh**oulish
sc: **sc**ythe, **sc**ene, **sc**epter, **sc**ience
rh: **rh**ythm, **rh**yme, **rh**etoric

Silent consonants also sometimes appear in the middle and at the end of a word. Here are some common examples:

bt: de**bt**, dou**bt**, su**bt**le
dg: lo**dg**ing, ju**dg**ment, tru**dg**e
ft: o**ft**en, so**ft**en
ght: ni**ght**, strai**ght**, fou**ght**
gn: forei**gn**, sovere**ign**, re**ign**
mn: autu**mn**, colu**mn**, hy**mn**
st: fa**st**en, moi**st**en, ne**st**le

Also, a few "solo" consonants are frequently silent. Consider these examples:

d: We**d**nesday
h: **h**erb, **h**our, **h**onor, shep**h**erd
l: ha**l**f, cha**l**k, Linco**l**n
p: cu**p**board, ra**sp**berry, cor**p**s

Before you learn the spelling rules covering other "soundless" spellings, let's test your skill with **silent vowels** and **silent consonants**.

Exercise 7.1

Use the phonetic spellings to correctly spell the following words in the space provided. Every word includes a silent **e** or a silent consonant.

1. RES-ul _____
2. RAYN _____
3. FAYL-yur _____
4. NOK _____
5. BLAYM _____
6. KAL-kyu-layt _____
7. AHN-ur-uh-bul _____
8. FUHJ _____
9. SAHL-um _____
10. LIS-un _____

Double Consonants

Another category of "silent" consonants is the *double* consonant—an identical pair of letters. In words with double consonants the sound of the second consonant cannot be distinguished. It lets the first consonant do the "talking" for both. **Chapter 3: Final Consonants** gives the rules for doubling a consonant at the end of a word when adding a suffix like **-ed** or **-ing**. However, there are many words with double consonants included in the root word. Here are the standard consonants and examples of words that include them:

bb: blu**bb**er, ca**bb**age, gi**bb**erish
cc: a**cc**ept, o**cc**upied, su**cc**ulent
dd: do**dd**er, sa**dd**le, u**dd**er
ff: su**ff**er, e**ff**igy, sni**ff**
gg: exa**gg**erate, ba**gg**age, go**gg**les
ll: ta**ll**ow, para**ll**el, a**ll**iance
mm: ma**mm**oth, fla**mm**able, reco**mm**end
nn: ma**nn**er, ca**nn**y, pe**nn**ant
pp: disa**pp**oint, a**pp**etite, a**pp**laud
rr: ma**rr**iage, emba**rr**ass, bu**rr**ow
ss: pre**ss**ure, care**ss**, la**ss**itude
tt: ti**tt**er, bu**tt**ress, le**tt**uce
zz: da**zz**le, si**zz**le, embe**zz**le

Letters in Disguise

Certain letter combinations "disguise" themselves in sounds that are completely different from the usual pronunciation of the separate letters. If you aren't careful, you can fall for the disguise and never notice that you've misspelled the word. Here are some of these troublesome letter combinations and the sounds they spell:

di:　the sound of **j** in **soldier** and **cordial**

j:　the sound of **y** in **hallelujah**

ge:　the sound of **zh** in **garage** and **mirage**

ph:　the sound of **f** in **sphere** and **photo**

ti/tu:　the sound of **ch** in **question** and **denture**

ti:　the sound of **sh** in **election** and **vibration**

x:　the sound of **z** in **xylophone**

Do this exercise to test your ability to correctly spell words with **double consonants** and **letters in disguise.**

Exercise 7.2

Use the phonetic spellings to correctly spell the following words in the space provided. Every word includes consonants or letters in disguise.

1. uh-TRAK-shun　　_____
2. b-LIJ-er-ent　　_____
3. HEM-is-feer　　_____
4. uh-PEER-ens　　_____
5. SIN-a-min　　_____
6. kuhl-LAZH　　_____
7. BOT-el　　_____
8. DIF-er-ent　　_____
9. sug-JES-tchun　　_____
10. suh-KUM　　_____

Chapter Mastery Test

Review the spelling rules you have learned in this chapter covering **silent letters.** Then complete the following questions to test your mastery of these spelling skills.

Part I: Fill in the silent or disguised consonant(s) in each of the following incomplete words.

1. an old family _____eirloom
2. a strike or wa_____kout
3. the pool hu_____ler
4. a sli_____ headache
5. a _____astly sight
6. the _____ent of perfume
7. _____owle_____e is not wisdom
8. an alias or _____eudonym
9. a cor_____ial greeting
10. the conde_____ed man
11. what man has _____ought
12. a burden of inde_____edness
13. glory hallelu_____ah
14. a frei_____ train
15. a _____inestone cowboy

Part II: Circle the *one* word that is correctly spelled in the following groups of words with double consonants.

1. nebbula　　rabble　　mobbile
2. vaccuum　　deccadent　　succotash
3. riddance　　proddigy　　iddealize
4. guffaw　　caffeteria　　profficient
5. sluggish　　proggress　　sufraggette
6. correllation　　stilleto　　infallible
7. dammage　　pummel　　ammoral

8.	connive	garnnish	tennant	12.	recittal	whittle	cuttlery

8. connive   garnnish   tennant
9. eppoch   appease   seeppage
10. chorral   durress   terrestrial
11. tissue   cressent   antissocial

12. recittal   whittle   cuttlery
13. drizzle   dezzert   azzure
14. eccentric muccous   deccade
15. omminous   mammary   ammendment

Core Word List #7

alien	cashier	financier	jewels	ninety
atheist	ceiling	friend	knowledge	perceive
attendance	chief	friendliness	laboratory	piece
attendant	deceitful	gaiety	leisure	proficient
attended	deceive	happiness	leisurely	relieve
author	dependent	hesitant	liveliest	tolerant
authoritative	entertain	ignorant	livelihood	view
authority	feign	influence	liveliness	violets
before	field	influential	lives	weird
careful	financially	involve	mischief	yield
careless				

Core Word Mastery Test

Master the spelling of these words from the core list and learn their meanings before you try to learn those in the chapters ahead. **Remember:** *In spelling, your goal is a perfect score.*

Part I: Insert **ie** or **ei** in the blank spaces.

1. Is the dog man's best fr_____nd?
2. Can you name the three w_____rd sisters in *Macbeth*?
3. The ath_____st denies the existence of God.
4. What is your ch_____f reason for refusing to attend the lecture?
5. Woman, arch dec_____ver of mankind.
6. I should like to lie in a f_____ld of clover.
7. Pierpont Morgan was one of Wall Street's greatest financ_____rs.
8. New Orleans's Mardi Gras is famed for its sprightly ga_____ty.
9. This summer I plan to relax and make full use of my l_____sure.
10. I cannot perc_____ve the difference between the two texts.
11. Look at that gigantic insect crawling across the c_____ling!
12. I want a room with a v_____w of the bay.
13. I will not y_____ld to pressure.
14. May I have another p_____ce of cake?
15. Aspirin may rel_____ve your headache.
16. I cannot f_____gn interest in your tale of woe any longer.

17. Zeno's unique perspective on life was completely al_____n to his colleagues'.
18. I'll fill the tank with gas while you go inside to pay the cash_____r.
19. I fear I shall never be profic_____nt in spelling.
20. Dennis, try not to get into any misch_____f while I'm gone.

Part II: Each of the core list words in the following sentences either *needs an additional letter* or *has an extra letter*. In either case, correct the spelling.

1. Financialy, I am in dire straits. More simply, I'm broke.
2. I intend to drive across the nation leisurly, stopping every few hours for a rest.
3. The courtroom atendant brought the prisoner before the bar.
4. I am seeking a definitive, authorittative opinion that will settle the problem.
5. We look befor and after and sigh for what is not.
6. Carless people make costly mistakes.
7. I have no knowlege of physics.
8. Once I worked in a chemical labratory as a test-tube cleaner.
9. I have, in my day, earned a livlihood as a dishwasher.
10. The car sped along at ninnety miles per hour.

11. What authorrity have you to enter my apartment without my permission?
12. Be carefull what you say about my mother-in-law.
13. Everyone wants a little hapiness in his life.
14. If you know an inffluential man, you may be able to get an apartment without waiting.
15. Livliness and wit may effectively replace physical beauty.

Part III: Proofread the following passage, correcting all spelling errors.

The authurs freindliness entertained those in attendence at the lecture. A few in the audience were hesatant to ask questions, since they were truly quite ignorent of his use of symbols. However, he was good-natured and tolrant of their awkward manners. Had their lifes been as involved as those of his factional characters, however (none of whom would have atended lectures of any kind), even his livliest manner would have failed to influance them. In truth, his characters seem to be dependant solely upon a sense of personal misery and failure. The author himself had been known to sucumb to a similarly negative outlook—but not that night!

CHAPTER EIGHT

Sound-Alike Words

This chapter contains an alphabetical glossary of words that are so similar in spelling or pronunciation (or both) that they are easily mistaken for each other. These words fall into two categories: homonyms and homophones.

o *Homonyms* are words that have the same pronunciation and spelling but different meanings. For example:

pole—a long shaft of wood
pole—one of two opposite points

o *Homophones* are words that have the same (or similar) pronunciation but different spellings and meanings. For example:

pole—a long shaft of wood
poll—a survey of public opinion

Obviously, these sound-alike words cause constant headaches for spellers. To help you learn to recognize the correct spelling for the word you *intend* to use, this chapter gives the part of speech and definition for every word. The exercises—generally following every *ten* sets of sound-alike words—give you practice using each word in context.

access	(noun) the right to enter or use; a means of approach
excess	(noun) amount greater than sufficient

accept	(verb) to take what is offered
except	(verb) to leave out; (conj.) only; (prep.) but
adjoin	(verb) to lie next to
adjourn	(verb) to suspend a session
adverse	(adj.) unfortunate; opposed
averse	(adj.) strong disliking, unwillingness
advice	(noun) an opinion, recommendation
advise	(verb) to offer an opinion
affect	(verb) to act upon; to influence
effect	(noun) result, consequence
aisle	(noun) passageway
isle	(noun) island
allowed	(verb) past tense of *to allow*
aloud	(adv.) with the voice, orally
alley	(noun) a narrow street or passageway
ally	(verb) to join in alliance; (noun) one joined in an alliance
all ready	(adj.) everything is ready
already	(adv.) before, previously
all together	(adj.) everyone in company
altogether	(adv.) completely

Exercise 8.1

Circle the correct word in each of the following sentences.

1. To win the contest, Bert had to swallow in [excess] [access] of 75 jalapeño peppers in a half hour.
2. Judy told the man she could never [except] [accept] a ride from a stranger.
3. The courtroom [adjoins] [adjourns] the judge's chambers.
4. Somehow he made it to shore, even though the hurricane had created [adverse] [averse] weather conditions.
5. Let me [advice] [advise] you to postpone your wedding until after the trial.
6. Some people are emotionally [affected] [effected] by the full moon.
7. She decided to elope rather than walk down the [aisle] [isle] of a church.
8. The lawyer read the will [allowed] [aloud] to the room of hopeful heirs.
9. [Ally] [Alley] yourself with me and we will conquer the block!
10. We [already] [all ready] told the driver that we would ride [altogether] [all together].

allusion	(noun) an indirect reference
illusion	(noun) a false impression; deception
altar	(noun) a table used for worship
alter	(verb) to change
angel	(noun) a celestial being
angle	(noun) a sharp corner; a geometric figure
ascent	(noun) an upward slope; a going upward
assent	(verb) to agree, consent
assistance	(noun) aid, help
assistants	(noun) those who give assistance, plural of *assistant*

berth (noun) a built-in bed on a vehicle; a place to dock

birth (noun) beginning, origin; fact of being born

beside (prep.) next to, at the side of

besides (adv.) in addition; otherwise

bloc (noun) a group with a common purpose, a coalition

block (noun) a solid piece of material; a unit of measurement

board (noun) a long, flat piece of wood

bored (noun) a feeling of dull weariness

boarder (noun) person who pays for meals and lodging

border (noun) an edge; a decorative rim

Exercise 8.2

Circle the correct word in each of the following sentences.

1. Sherwood was under the [allusion] [illusion] that Sophie would go with him.
2. Marvin will have to [altar] [alter] his attitude before his boss will give him a promotion.
3. Her temper is sharp, but otherwise she's as sweet as an [angle] [angel].
4. Stephen would never [assent] [ascent] to climb the mountain when he could ride instead.
5. I need some [assistants] [assistance] carrying these packages upstairs.
6. An early silent epic movie was *[Berth] [Birth] of a Nation.*
7. We had hoped to rest here, [beside] [besides] needing to eat.
8. The countries in the Communist [block] [bloc] are experiencing upheaval.
9. Jane complained that she was [bored] [board] with no one to play with.
10. The outlaw made a desperate run for the Mexican [boarder] [border].

brake (noun) device for slowing or stopping motion

break (verb) to split into pieces

breath (noun) air inhaled and exhaled

breathe (verb) to inhale and exhale air

bridal (noun) relating to a bride or wedding

bridle (noun) head gear used to control a horse

Britain (noun) a country, the kingdom of Great Britain

Briton (noun) an Englishman, living in Great Britain

Calvary (noun) hill near Jerusalem where Jesus was crucified

cavalry (noun) soldiers mounted on horses

canvas (noun) a heavy, coarse cloth

canvass (verb) to conduct a survey; to discuss thoroughly

capital (noun) city that is official seat of government; money

capitol (noun) building in which body of government meets

censor (noun) person who removes morally questionable material from written and performed works

censure (verb) to criticize strongly, blame; (noun) official criticism

chord (noun) combination of notes

cord (noun) a small rope; a feeling or force that connects

cite (verb) to quote or refer to an authority

sight (noun) a view; (verb) to see, to aim

site (noun) place or setting, location

Exercise 8.3

Circle the correct word in each of the following sentences.

1. If you aren't careful, she will [break] [brake] your heart.
2. Feeling dizzy, she began to [breath] [breathe] slowly and deeply.
3. Goodwin grabbed the [bridal] [bridle] and began to lead the mare to her stall.
4. No respectable [Briton] [Britain] drinks coffee at teatime.
5. She wept when the tour bus drove past the historical site known as [Cavalry] [Calvary].
6. We [canvased] [canvassed] the neighborhood about the proposed traffic light.
7. Architects have been hired to renovate the state [capital] [capitol].
8. The committee angrily [censured] [censored] Magda for nude dancing.
9. The beautiful music created a shared [chord] [cord] of feeling between us.
10. The ground-breaking ceremony will take place at the [sight] [site] of the new courthouse.

climactic (adj.) related to the most intense or noteworthy point

climatic (adj.) related to the weather

cloths (noun-plural) pieces of material

clothes (noun-plural) garments, wearing apparel

coarse (adj.) unrefined; rough

course (noun) path; direction; a unit of study

complement (noun) something that completes; (verb) to complete

compliment (noun) an expression of praise; (verb) to praise

correspondence (noun) letters written or received; the exchange of letters

correspondents (noun) people who communicate by letter, plural of *correspondent*

core (noun) the innermost or most important part

corps (noun) a group following the same purpose or leadership

council	(noun) group of people organized to consider matters
counsel	(noun) advice; (verb) to advise
crochet	(noun) a form of needlework; (verb) to do that needlework
crotchet	(noun) an odd or stubborn notion
croquet	(noun) a lawn game played with wooden balls and mallets
croquette	(noun) a small cake of minced food
currant	(noun) a small, dried seedless grape
current	(adj.) now in progress, presently the case

Exercise 8.4

Circle the correct word in each of the following sentences.

1. The [climatic] [climactic] point of the storm occurred when lightning struck the mast.
2. The [clothes] [cloths] in that bucket are cleaning rags.
3. His skin was [coarse] [course] from working outdoors.
4. That silk rose is the perfect [compliment] [complement] for your outfit.
5. Rosalie regularly receives [correspondents] [correspondence] from her pen pals in Russia and Nicaragua.
6. He intended to join the medical [corps] [core] but went into electronics instead.
7. Running Bear gave wise [council] [counsel] to the young braves on the reservation.
8. She was an eccentric old woman who was full of strange [crochets] [crotchets].
9. My mother's favorite meal is salmon [croquet] [croquette] with a Dijon mustard sauce.
10. His [currant] [current] hobby is making dried fruit.

dairy	(noun) a farm where milk is produced commercially
diary	(noun) a personal journal, record of events
deprecate	(verb) to disapprove, belittle
depreciate	(verb) to lessen the price or value of a thing or person
decent	(adj.) meeting accepted standards
descent	(noun) act of going downward, descending
dissent	(verb) to disagree; (noun) disagreement
desert	(noun) a dry, barren region; (verb) to leave, abandon
dessert	(noun) sweet food served at the end of a meal
device	(noun) something made for a particular purpose
devise	(verb) to plan, invent, make
die	(verb) to stop living
dye	(noun) something used to color material; (verb) to color

dining	(verb) present participle of *to dine*
dinning	(verb) present participle of *to din*
dual	(adj.) having two parts, double
duel	(noun) formal combat between two people
elicit	(verb) to bring out
illicit	(adj.) unlawful
emigrant	(noun) one who leaves one country to live in another
immigrant	(noun) one who enters one country after leaving another

Exercise 8.5

Circle the correct word in each of the following sentences.

1. The modern [diary] [dairy] is more like a factory than a farm.
2. Marlon constantly [deprecates] [depreciates] his wife's ability as a housekeeper.
3. Our [decent] [descent] was much faster after our car brakes failed.
4. "Don't [dessert] [desert] me," sobbed the soap opera heroine.
5. Audrey will [device] [devise] a way to get revenge on her little brother.
6. She would rather [die] [dye] than admit she's not a natural blonde.
7. Sloppy Joe's Cafe isn't known for fine [dining] [dinning], but no one has died of food poisoning yet.
8. Do you know which American president once fought a [duel] [dual]?
9. If torture won't [illicit] [elicit] the answer, then maybe bribery will.
10. Except for the native Indians, all Americans can be considered [immigrants] [emigrants].

eminent	(adj.) prominent, outstanding, distinguished
imminent	(adj.) about to occur, impending
ensure	(verb) to make sure, certain
insure	(verb) to protect against loss with insurance
envelop	(verb) to enclose, wrap around completely
envelope	(noun) a flat, folded paper container
faint	(verb) to lose consciousness; (adj.) lacking strength or courage
feint	(verb) to make a quick, misleading movement
flair	(noun) a natural talent
flare	(verb) to burn with sudden brightness
formally	(adj.) in a formal manner
formerly	(adv.) at a previous time; once
forth	(adv.) onward; out into view
fourth	(noun) number after *third*; one of four equal parts
foul	(adj.) offensive to the sense or the morals
fowl	(noun) a bird; the meat of a bird

gait   (noun) a manner of moving on foot

gate   (noun) a movable device at the entrance to a passageway

hear   (verb) to perceive by ear

here   (adv.) at this place or time

Exercise 8.6

Circle the correct word in each of the following sentences.

1. Professor Zbgnwsk is [imminent] [eminent] in the field of computer languages.
2. You must [ensure] [insure] that no one else learns about this.
3. Grampa will [envelope] [envelop] all four children in one long-armed hug.
4. Dan [feinted] [fainted] to the left and then punched Roy hard in the jaw.
5. She has a [flare] [flair] for cake decoration.
6. You'd never suspect he was [formally] [formerly] a millionaire.
7. Abraham was the [fourth] [forth] of eighteen children.
8. The open refrigerator filled the kitchen with a [fowl] [foul] smell.
9. You could tell Uncle Hans was a sailor from his rolling [gate] [gait].
10. From the sound of it, the train will be [hear] [here] any minute.

heard   (verb) past tense of *to hear*

herd   (noun) a group of cattle or similar animals; a crowd

heir   (noun) one who inherits

air   (noun) a mixture of breathable gases

heroin   (noun) a narcotic drug

heroine   (noun) a woman known for courage or achievements

hoard   (verb) to gather a hidden supply; (noun) a hidden supply

horde   (noun) a large group, crowd, swarm

hostel   (noun) an inexpensive lodging, an inn

hostile   (adj.) unfriendly; against

idle   (adj.) doing nothing; not in use

idol   (noun) a false god

incidence   (noun) the frequency of occurrence

incidents   (noun) events, occurrences, plural of *incident*

ingenious   (adj.) clever, imaginative

ingenuous   (adj.) simple, forthright, unsophisticated

instance   (noun) example; episode

instants   (noun) moments, plural of *instant*

its   (pronoun) the possessive of *it*

it's   contraction of *it is*

Exercise 8.7

Circle the correct word in each of the following sentences.

1. The museum guides direct the [heards] [herds] of visitors through as quickly as possible.
2. The next generation will be [airs] [heirs] of a spoiled planet.
3. Although it has positive uses, [heroin] [heroine] has had a negative effect on society.
4. In the attic he came across a [horde] [hoard] of comic books.
5. Fire ants are [hostel] [hostile] to all birds that nest on the ground.
6. His hands were [idle] [idol], but his imagination wasn't.
7. The [incidence] [incidents] of kissing among teenagers is high.
8. Matthew's [ingenuous] [ingenious] manner inspired trust among us.
9. The food fight is only one [instants] [instance] of his behavior problem.
10. The dog chased [it's] [its] own tail and finally caught it.

later	(adv.) after the expected time
latter	(adj.) the second of two persons or things mentioned previously
lead	(noun) a heavy metal
led	(verb) past tense of *to lead*
lessen	(verb) to make less; to become less
lesson	(noun) something to be learned
liable	(adj.) likely; legally responsible
libel	(noun) a damaging statement about a person

lightning	(noun) an electrical flash in the sky
lightening	(verb) present participle of *to lighten*
loan	(noun) something lent temporarily
lone	(adj.) without company; the only one
loose	(adj.) not tightly fastened; (verb) to release, undo
lose	(verb) to be unable to find; to no longer have
maybe	(adv.) perhaps
may be	(aux./verb) indicates possibility
miner	(noun) person who takes minerals from the earth
minor	(adj.) lesser in amount, importance, or seriousness; (noun) a child
missal	(noun) a prayer book
missile	(noun) a weapon that is thrown or dropped

Exercise 8.8

Circle the correct word in each of the following sentences.

1. Both television and newspapers covered the facts, but the [latter] [later] gave you the real story.
2. The tunnel [lead] [led] to an underground cavern.
3. Your kindness cannot [lessen] [lesson] her loneliness.

4. If you don't watch out, that dog is [liable] [libel] to nip your ankle.
5. His bright smile is [lightening] [lightning] her last days on earth.
6. The hill is bare except for a [lone] [loan] pine tree on the western slope.
7. Put the door key in your shoe so you won't [lose] [loose] it.
8. She may go with us, but [may be] [maybe] she won't.
9. Jeff's "big catastrophe" turned out to be only a [minor] [miner] problem.
10. The preacher threw his [missal] [missile] on the floor in disgust.

moral	(adj.) ethical, relating to right conduct
morale	(noun) attitude, level of confidence and enthusiasm
muscle	(noun) tissue that carries out bodily movement
mussel	(noun) a bivalve, like a clam
naval	(adj.) relating to the navy or ships
navel	(noun) small scar on the belly of mammals
passed	(verb) past tense of *to pass*
past	(adj.) over; no longer current
patience	(noun) calm endurance
patients	(noun) people under medical treatment, plural of *patient*
peace	(noun) the absence of war or disturbance
piece	(noun) a portion

peddle	(verb) to travel about selling goods
pedal	(noun) a lever worked by the foot
petal	(noun) a segment of a flower
personal	(adj.) relating to a particular person
personnel	(noun) people employed by an organization
peal	(verb) to ring loudly; (noun) a loud burst of noise
peel	(verb) to remove the skin; (noun) piece of removed skin
presence	(noun) the fact of being present; a person's bearing
presents	(noun) gifts, plural of *present*

Exercise 8.9

Circle the correct word in each of the following sentences.

1. Team [morale] [moral] was high before the big game.
2. You will build up [mussel] [muscle] mass by lifting weights.
3. The tour bus stopped next at the [navel] [naval] museum.
4. In the [passed] [past] millions of buffalo roamed the American plains.
5. The nurse cared for him with gentleness and [patients] [patience].
6. Some people believe mankind is too warlike to ever know real [peace] [piece].
7. In Paris vendors [peddle] [pedal] flowers in huge carts on the streets.
8. In the last year we have more than doubled our [personnel] [personal].

9. Should I [peal] [peel] the potatoes or slice the onions?
10. Our [presents] [presence] is required at a family meeting after dinner.

principal	(adj.) first or foremost in importance, chief
principle	(noun) basic rule of conduct or action
quiet	(adj.) making no noise; still
quit	(verb) to stop; to leave
quite	(adv.) completely; actually
rain	(noun) water falling to earth in drops
rein	(noun) device used to guide a horse; (verb) to hold back, to control
reign	(noun) rule of a monarch; (verb) to rule
raise	(verb) to lift up; to move upward; to set upright
raze	(verb) to tear down, demolish
respectfully	(adv.) showing proper respect
respectively	(adv.) single, each in turn
review	(verb) to study; to look back on
revue	(noun) a musical variety show
right	(adj.) correct; (noun) something due by law or tradition
rite	(noun) a ceremony
write	(verb) to form letters or words on a surface; to compose

road	(noun) a wide path for vehicles, people, and animals
rode	(verb) past tense of *to ride*
role	(noun) a part, function, or position filled by someone
roll	(noun) a small rounded portion of bread; (verb) to revolve
sail	(noun) fabric designed to propel a boat by catching wind
sale	(noun) availability for purchase; the transaction of selling

Exercise 8.10

Circle the correct word in each of the following sentences.

1. *A* is the [principle] [principal] letter in the English alphabet.
2. Are you [quit] [quite] sure you want both lemon *and* milk in your tea?
3. Jerome struggled to [reign] [rein] in his temper.
4. Earthquakes literally [raised] [razed] the entire country of Armenia.
5. It took two hours for the fifty award winners to [respectively] [respectfully] cross the stage and receive their plaques.
6. He [revued] [reviewed] the events of the past week with amazement.
7. Everyone has the [rite] [right] to refuse, but often we forget to use it.
8. Mrs. Boswell [road] [rode] the train because she was afraid of planes.

9. Churchill played a very important [roll] [role] during the war.
10. He insists that his Elvis record collection is not for [sale] [sail].

serge	(noun) a fabric often used to make suits
surge	(verb) to increase suddenly; to move like waves
shear	(verb) to cut off
sheer	(adj.) straight up and down; thin, almost transparent
shone	(verb) past tense of *to shine*
shown	(verb) past tense of *to show*
soar	(verb) to fly high, with ease
sore	(adj.) painful, hurting
stationary	(adj.) not moving
stationery	(noun) writing paper and envelopes
statue	(noun) a likeness made of stone, clay, wood, or bronze
stature	(noun) natural upright height; status
straight	(adj.) not curved or crooked
strait	(noun) a narrow passage of water; a difficult position
tail	(noun) the rear end of a thing or animal
tale	(noun) a story
taught	(verb) past tense of *to teach*
taut	(adj.) pulled or drawn tight; tense
team	(noun) a group organized to work together
teem	(verb) to be full of

Exercise 8.11

Circle the correct word in each of the following sentences.

1. My grandfather wore his blue [surge] [serge] suit only on Sundays.
2. Wild waves crashed against the [sheer] [shear] cliff.
3. His eyes [shone] [shown] with love as he held his infant son.
4. Clint's back is [sore] [soar] from moving furniture.
5. Although we were [stationery] [stationary], the wind gave us the sensation of movement.
6. Standing at full [statue] [stature], the basketball player towered over us.
7. He's managed to get himself into financially desperate [straits] [straights].
8. The funniest part was when he caught his coat [tale] [tail] in the door.
9. The muscles in his back were [taught] [taut] with the strain.
10. One drop of water [teams] [teems] with microscopic life.

than	(conj.) used to introduce the second item in a comparison
then	(adv.) at that time in the past
their	(pronoun) the possessive of *they*
there	(adv.) at or in that place or time
they're	contraction of *they are*

threw	(verb) past tense of *to throw*
through	(prep.) from one side to the other; finished
to	(prep.) in a direction toward
too	(adv.) more than enough; also
two	(noun) the number after one
vain	(adj.) excessively proud; unsuccessful
vein	(noun) blood vessel; an underlying quality, streak
vane	(noun) a device that moves to show wind direction
veracious	(adj.) honest, truthful
voracious	(adj.) having a strong appetite, greedy
vial	(noun) a small container for liquids
vile	(adj.) unpleasant, disgusting
waist	(noun) the mid-line of the body or of a garment
waste	(noun) garbage, trash; (verb) to use carelessly, squander

Exercise 8.12

Circle the correct word in each of the following sentences.

1. It's colder [then] [than] an iceberg in here!
2. If you ask me, [they're] [their] just trying to get attention.
3. When she finished the race, she [through] [threw] her hat in the air.
4. One can never be [to] [too] rich.
5. Stella has a [vain] [vein] of meanness running through her.
6. Nick is quite [vane] [vain] about his thick blond hair.
7. Despite his [voracious] [veracious] appetite, he stays thin.
8. After two months in the refrigerator the fruit salad was [vile] [vial].
9. It is tragic to watch Paula [waist] [waste] her singing talent in the shower.

wait	(verb) to be inactive or stay in one place
weight	(noun) measure of heaviness
weak	(adj.) lacking strength or energy
week	(noun) seven days
weather	(noun) the state of the atmosphere
whether	(conj.) introduces an alternative
were	(verb) second person singular past tense of *to be*.
we're	contraction of *we are*
where	(adv.) at or in what place
which	(adj.) the one or ones indicated
witch	(noun) a woman who practices magic
whose	(pronoun) the possessive of *who*
who's	contraction of *who is*
your	(pronoun) the possessive of *you*
you're	contraction of *you are*

Exercise 8.13

Circle the correct word in each of the following sentences.

1. The [weight] [wait] seemed to last for hours.
2. Ruth grew [weak] [week] from her strict diet.
3. I'm going to climb that mountain, [weather] [whether] you like it or not!
4. Anita and Jorge [where] [were] on the tables, dancing the flamenco.
5. In two weeks [were] [we're] going to California.
6. On Halloween [which] [witch] costume will you wear?
7. Frankie is watching the man [whose] [who's] car is parked over there.
8. If [your] [you're] going to town, can I hitch a ride?

Chapter Mastery Test

Review the spelling rules you have learned in this chapter covering **sound-alike words**. Then complete the following questions to test your spelling mastery of these words.

In the following paragraphs circle the misspelled sound-alike words and write the correct spelling for each in the space provided below.

1. According to most modern books on etiquette, members of the bridle party fill an important roll before and during the wedding. On the day of the wedding itself, they must provide a number of personnel services. Weather its recording presence in the bride's book or shaking out rumpled cloths, bridesmaids must be prepared to handle every chore with cheerful patients. Not only that, they must support the bride's moral with complements and encouragement. After all, she reins as queen that day. And her throne is the alter.

_____
_____
_____
_____
_____

2. For a pleasant dinning experience, garnish your foods attractively. When serving foul, place several thin slices of orange peal upon each peace. With fish croquets, you can achieve a charming affect with a lose scattering of currents or other small fruit. And don't forget desert! For pies and cakes, create a decorative boarder of rose pedals. When everything is already, serve your meal with flare.

_____
_____
_____
_____
_____

3.   The coach wanted to get his teem in shape before football season began, and he knew he had a big job on his hands. The players had let their mussels get week and their wastes get thick. Everyone had put on two much wait. He warned everyone that he was going to work their tales off, than told them to start running laps. On the forth lap, a few players complained that they couldn't breath, but their complaints were in vane. On the tenth lap, one feinted. The next day, however, the only averse result was some miner soarness.

_____

_____

_____

_____

4.   As Khan lead his hostel hoards toward the city of Burg, the town counsel met to decide on a coarse of action. Some argued that the town should simply surrender and except Khan as ruler. But others reminded them of the stories about Khan, the many incidence of brutality and cruelty that had been reported. "Also," they said, "we cannot abandon our alley, the neighboring town of Hamlet." Finally, they came up with a devise that would launch a deadly missal strait into the ranks of the invading core. Khan certainly learned his lessen!

_____

_____

_____

_____

5.   To rule well, a leader must base all his actions upon principal. His statue among his countrymen should depend upon his treating them respectively and voraciously. History has shone that the greatest leaders illicited the very best from their followers and razed them to greater heights of personnel dignity. Such leaders taut that power was a tool and excess to power a rite of all the people. Great rulers have no allusions about the reasons for their assent to imminence.

_____

_____

_____

_____

Core Word List #8

accompanied	carried	connote	extremely	scissors
accompanies	carrier	consummate	innuendo	sincerely
accompaniment	carries	council	malicious	stories
accompanying	carrying	counsel	omit	story
advantage	changeable	counselor	omitted	strictly
advantageous	changing	countries	parallel	sufficient
applies	commissioner	curable	particular	swimming
applying	companies	desirability	passage	theories
buried	company	desire	permit	theory
bury	connotation	dilettante	recognize	transferred

Core Word Mastery Test

Master the spelling of these words from the core list and learn their meanings before you try to learn those in the chapters ahead. **Remember:** *In spelling, your goal is a perfect score.*

Part I: In each of the core list words in the following sentences, a blank space has been left for *one* letter. Add the appropriate letter.

1. Will Joe be carr_____ing your books this afternoon?
2. Send the water carr_____er on to the field.
3. I question the desir_____bility of visiting him at this time.
4. He has been extrem_____ly ill for several weeks.
5. The countess was accompan_____ed by her husband.
6. It is always advantag_____ous to buy two books for the price of one.
7. What I say to your brother appl_____es to you as well.
8. He is a man of extremely chang_____able moods.
9. How many compan_____es went into bankruptcy last year?
10. I have been counting the number of countr_____es in Western Europe.

Part II: Some of the core list words in the following sentences require *single* consonants; some require *double* consonants. In the space provided, write the appropriate number of consonants.

Example: He is fi_____ing the cup. (consonant: l) Answer: *filling.*
Example: He is fi_____ing his nails. (consonant: l) Answer: *filing.*

1. You have omi_____ed two questions from your answer paper. (t)
2. Will you go swi_____ing with me this afternoon? (m)
3. The prospectors searched for the bu_____ied gold. (r)
4. The policeman was transfe_____ed to a new precinct. (r)
5. Two lines running exactly beside one

another are called
para_____e_____. (l)

6. The word "Mom" co_____otes a richer emotional tone than the word "Mother." (n)

7. Will your sister be a_____ompanying you to the dance? (c)

8. The groom ca_____ied his bride across the threshold. (r)

9. If I am called to trial, I shall ask my counse_____or to represent me. (l)

10. Two spoonfuls of sugar will be su_____icient for my tea. (f)

11. The teenage newlyweds were caught by their parents before they could consu_____ate the marriage. (m)

12. Is her disease cu_____able or fatal? (r)

13. Stefan has never achieved true success because he is merely a dile_____ante. (t)

14. She undermines his efforts with poisonous i_____uendo. (n)

15. Many daring explorers lost their lives searching for the Northwest Pa_____age. (s)

Part III: Circle the *one* correctly spelled choice in the following sentences.

1. Lobbyists are most [particlar] [particular] about the congressmen they buttonhole.

2. Machinists are more effective with practical matters than with [theory's] [theories].

3. Numismatists recount exciting [stories] [storys] about the coins they have collected.

4. Optometrists listen [sincerly] [sincerely] to their patients' visual problems.

5. Politicians suffer from an inability to avoid words whose [connotations] [conotations] arouse feeling rather than reflective thought.

6. Quail breeders are always watching to determine when their male stock needs [changeing] [changing].

7. Radio announcers spend their leisure time [applieing] [applying] for jobs in television.

8. Soloists in symphony orchestras rely upon intelligent [accompanyment] [accompaniment] from their colleagues.

9. Tailors specialize in stitching what their customers [dessire] [desire].

10. Upholsterers often like to work in [commpany] [company] with tack pullers.

11. When his ambitions are frustrated, Edwin can be quite [malicious] [malecious].

12. The police [comissioner] [commissioner] is keeping a low profile since the scandal broke.

13. She has both pruning shears and embroidery [siscors] [scissors].

14. All officer candidates must [strickly] [strictly] abide by the honor code.

15. Your name is familiar, but I don't [recognize] [recongize] your face.

Part IV: Proofread the following passage, correcting all errors in spelling.

Sometimes a newspaper editor will burry or ommit a storry—and the picture that accompanys it—that carrys references that do not show his favorite thoery to addvantage. Without avail, a counsel of his fellow editors often council him not to permet his prejudice to corrupt his judgment.

PART THREE

PUTTING THE PARTS TOGETHER

CHAPTER NINE

Root Words

The root of a word is like its spine—it provides the central backbone of meaning to which prefixes and suffixes can attach like arms and legs. No matter what kind of "direction" or "activity" a prefix or suffix brings to a word, without the *root* to provide a "center of gravity," the word can go nowhere and do nothing. Consider the following group of words with the Latin root **fac**, meaning "make" or "do."

o **fac**t—that which is already *done* (a deed or act)
o **fac**tory—a place where things are *made* (a plant where items are manu**fac**tured)
o **fac**tor—one who *does* or *makes* things for someone else (a merchant or agent) or, in another sense, a *fact* that *makes* things what they are (a circumstance or condition)
o **fac**tion—a clique that *does* things together (a partisan group)
o **fac**totum—an all-around man hired to *do* all sorts of jobs (a handyman)

You can combine **fac** with other roots to create additional words: Add **simile** (like) and you get **facsimile**—"that which is made like something else" (a reproduction). Add **manu** (hand) and you get **manufacture**—"that which is made by hand." The single root **fac** produces more than one hundred English words.

Here's another example with the Latin root **fin**, meaning "boundary":

o **fin**ish—to arrive at the *boundary* (to come to the end)
o **fin**ite—having *bounds* (measurable)
o in**fin**ite—having no *bounds* (unmeasurable)
o de**fin**e—placing *boundaries* around (to give precise meaning)
o de**fin**ite—precisely *bounded* (specific, having precise limits)

Being familiar with root words gives you the power to understand the meaning of words that are unfamiliar—and to *spell* them correctly. The greatest number of roots in English derive from the classical languages, Latin and Greek. There are about 160 Latin and Greek roots in English—but you need not learn them all. By learning the most common roots, you can build your vocabulary *and* increase your spelling mastery at the same time.

The following list includes most of the Latin and Greek roots used in English, their meanings, and a sampling of words that include them. Asterisks mark the roots that are most common—and therefore those that would be most useful to memorize. The original language of each root is indicated by a capital letter in parentheses—(L) for Latin and (G) for Greek. Use the list as a resource to help you expand your vocabulary and strengthen your spelling skills. Once you master the root words—and the suffixes and prefixes in the next two chapters—you will be able to build whole families of words:

Root	Meaning	English Words
aesth (G)	feel, perceive	aesthetics, esthete, anesthetic
agog (G)	lead, bring	demagogue, synagogue
agon (G)	contest, struggle	protagonist, antagonist, agony
am (L)	love	amorous, amatory, amour
***anim** (L)	mind, soul, life	animal, animate, unanimous
anthrop (G)	man	anthropology, misanthrope
***arch** (G)	rule, govern	anarchy, archives, archetype
aster (G)	star	asterisk, astronomy, disaster
***auto** (G)	self	autobiography, automatic, autopsy
bell (L—*bellus*)	beautiful, fair	belle, belles-lettres
bell (L—*bellum*)	war	bellicose, belligerent, rebel
bibl (G)	book	bible, bibliography
bio (G)	life	biology, biography, symbiotic
***cap, cip, cept** (L)	take, hold	capable, captivate, anticipate, principal, accept, deception
***ced, cess** (L)	go, yield	succeed, recede, process, excess
cent (L)	hundred	century, centennial
chron (G)	time	chronicle, chronic, chronology, synchronize
cit (L)	summon, arouse	recite, excite, cite, incite
civ (L)	citizen	civic, civilization, civil, civilian
cognit (L)	know	cognizant, incognito, cognition
cor, cord (L)	heart	accord, concord, discord, cordial, courage
corp (L)	body	corpse, corporal, corporation
cred (L)	believe, credit	discredit, credible, incredulous
culp (L)	offense, fault	culprit, culpable
cur, curs (L)	run	current, concourse, precursor, cursory
dem (G)	people	democrat, demagogue, epidemic, endemic

Root	Meaning	English Words
dexter (L)	right hand	dexterous, ambidextrous
*dic, dict (L)	say, speak	dictate, contradict, dedicate
dign (L)	worthy	dignify, condign, indignity
duc, duce (L)	lead, bring	induce, deduce, product, conduit
dur (L)	hard	duress, endure, obdurate
dynam (G)	power	dynamic, aerodynamics, dynamite
*fac, fact, fect (L)	do, make, act	facsimile, faction, effect, perfect
fall (L)	deceive, err	fallacy, fallacious, infallible
*ferr, fer (L)	carry, bring	ferry, infer, refer, fertile
ferv (L)	boil	fervid, effervesce, fervor
fin (L)	boundary	finish, infinite, define, confine
gam (G)	marriage	monogamy, bigamy, amalgam
geo (G)	earth	geography, geology, geometry
*gen, gener (L)	class, kind, race	general, engender, generic
*grad, gress (L)	walk, go, step	gradual, graduate, digress, transgress
graph (G)	write	autograph, biography, phonograph
grand (L)	great	aggrandize, grandiose, grandeur
homo (G)	the same	homogenized, homonym, homogeneous
idios (G)	one's own	idiom, idiosyncrasy, idiot
isos (G)	equal	isosceles, isotope, isobar
it (L)	go	exit, circuit, itinerant
ject (L)	throw, hurl	eject, deject, inject, reject
jur (L)	swear	jury, abjure, perjure
kosm (G)	universe, order	cosmic, cosmetic, cosmopolitan
krat (G)	power	democracy, aristocrat, bureaucrat
labor (L)	work	laboratory, collaborate, laborious
*log (G)	word, speak, science	logic, eulogy, tautology, archaeology, physiology
loqu, loc (L)	talk, speak	elocution, loquacious, grandiloquent, soliloquy, colloquial
*medi (L)	middle	medieval, mediate, medium
meta (G)	change	metamorphosis, metabolism, metaphor
meter, metr (G)	measure	diameter, symmetry, metronome
*mit, miss, mise (L)	send, throw	emit, submit, permission, dismiss demise, surmise
mon, monit (L)	warn, advise, remind	premonition, admonition, monument
mon, mono (G)	alone	monogamy, monolith, monogram
mor, mort (L)	death	mortal, immortal, mortician, mortify
nasc, nat (L)	to be born	natal, nature, renaissance
neo (G)	new	neolithic, neophyte, neologism

Root	Meaning	English Words
neur (G)	nerve, tendon	neuralgia, neuritis, neurotic
nom (G)	law	economy, Deuteronomy
nomin (L)	name	nomenclature, nominate, ignominious
nov (L)	new	innovate, novice, renovate, novelty
omni (L)	all	omniscient, omnipotent, omnibus
onym (G)	name	pseudonym, anonymous, homonym
ortho (G)	correct	orthodox, orthodontics
parl (L)	speak	parliament, parley, parlance, parlor
path (G)	feeling	sympathy, apathetic, antipathy
phil (G)	loving, fond, friendly	philanthropist, philosophy, philharmonic
phone (G)	sound	phonetic, telephone, phonology, euphony
physi (G)	nature	physiology, physicist, physiognomy
plic (L)	twine, twist	explicate, complicate, implicate
polis (G)	city	metropolis, politician, police, policy
pondu (L)	weight	ponderous, imponderable, preponderance
*****port** (L)	carry, bring, bear	portable, export, important
proto (G)	earliest, first	proton, protocol, protoplasm, protoype
psyche (G)	mind	psychic, psychotic, psychiatry
pyr (G)	fire	pyre, pyromaniac, pyrotechnics
rap, rapt (L)	seize, grasp	rape, rapture, rapacious
scop (G)	see	scope, telescope, microscope
*****sed, sess** (L)	sit	sedentary, reside, sediment
soph (G)	wise	sophomore, sophisticate, philosophy
*****spec, spect, spic** (L)	look, see, appear	species, spectacle, conspicuous
*****string, strict, strain** (L)	bind, draw tight	stringent, constrict, restrain
tang (L)	touch	tangible, intangible, contact, tangent
tele (G)	far	telescope, telegraph, telepathy
*****ten, tin, tain** (L)	hold	tenable, tenure, content, pertinent, detain, maintain
therm (G)	heat	thermal, thermometer, thermostat
top (G)	a place	topography, topic, topical
tort, torq (L)	twist	distort, tortuous, retort, contortion
tract (L)	draw	attract, detract, traction, protract
typ (G)	model	typical, archetype, atypical
*****vers, vert** (L)	turn	avert, extravert, aversion, adversary
vir (L)	man	virile, virtuous, virago
*****voc, vok** (L)	call	convoke, evoke, vocalize, advocate
vol (L)	wish	volition, malevolent, voluntary
zo (G)	animal	zoo, zoology, zodiac, protozoa

Chapter Mastery Test

When you are familiar with the most common **root words** (those marked by an asterisk), complete the following questions to test your spelling mastery.

Part I: Match each root with its original meaning.

_____ 1. medi   a. look, see, appear
_____ 2. cess   b. go, step
_____ 3. spect   c. go, yield
_____ 4. anim   d. carry, bring
_____ 5. voc   e. middle
_____ 6. port   f. take, hold
_____ 7. cap   g. call
_____ 8. auto   h. hold
_____ 9. grad   i. self
_____10. tain   j. mind, soul, life

Part II: In the space provided, fill in the missing root for each word in the following groups. A list of possible roots is given for each group.

A. port fac gener gress arch miss
  1. o_____ion
  2. _____ate

  3. hier_____y
  4. trans_____
  5. ag_____ion

B. voc auto dict log spec fer
  6. _____abulary
  7. suf_____
  8. _____imen
  9. _____nomous
 10. pre_____

C. port capa fac strict anim vers
 11. _____osity
 12. re_____
 13. _____ility
 14. _____city
 15. contro_____y

D. cip log sed mise medi cede
 16. pro_____ue
 17. parti_____ate
 18. se_____
 19. im_____ate
 20. _____ation

Core Word List #9

accomplish	alleviate	continuous	planned	stabilization
accuracy	allocate	crises	plausible	stigma
accurate	allotment	crisis	pleasant	susceptible
accurately	allotted	demonstrable	possible	those
admission	allow	deplorable	quantity	thought
admit	allowed	ignoble	religion	tomorrow
admittance	allows	medicinal	response	tremendous
afraid	altar	medieval	significance	undoubtedly
against	amateur	paid	speech	vengeance
aggravate	concede	physical	sponsor	warrant

Core Word Mastery Test

Master the spelling of these words from the core list and learn their meanings before you try to learn those in the chapters ahead.

Remember: *In spelling, your goal is a perfect score.*

Part I: Match the core list word in *Column B* with the appropriate context in *Column A*. If the core list word is misspelled, correct it.

Column A

1. This will relieve the pain.
2. We strive to avoid price fluctuation.
3. I yield to your argument.
4. He wants his share.
5. Your facts are entirely right.
6. He has no professional status.
7. Will he underwrite our venture?
8. He is disposed toward illness.
9. Don't make it worse.
10. What meaning does that sentence have?

Column B

a. conseed
b. sponser
c. acurate
d. aggrevate
e. aleviate
f. amatoor
g. stabilisation
h. suseptible
i. significence
j. allottment

Part II: In the space provided, write the correct word choice for each sentence.

1. The rain on the plain in Spain last year was _____ .
   (continnuous, continuous, continueous)
2. We hope at last to be _____ on time.
   (payed, payd, paid)
3. The Army asked each man to submit to a _____ examination.
   (physical, pysical, phisical)
4. You will _____ pass your intelligence tests.
   (undoubtedly, undoubtdely, undoubttedly)
5. _____ in spelling is prerequisite to success in business.
   (Acuracy, Accuraccy, Accuracy)
6. I tried without success to gain _____ to the ball.
   (admittance, admitance, admittence)
7. How much rice has been _____ to the needy people of Korea?
   (alotted, alloted, allotted)
8. _____ creeps in this petty pace from day to day.
   (Tommorrow, Tomorrow, Tommorow)
9. A heavyweight boxer has a _____ weight advantage over a flyweight.
   (tremendous, tremenjus, tremendius)

10. The police issued a _____ for the arrest of the escaped arsonist. (warrent, warant, warrant)
11. As emergency room nurse, I've seen more than my share of _____ . (crisises, crises, crise's)
12. Matilda's talents are _____ , but then so are her character flaws. (demonstrible, demmonstrable, demonstrable)
13. His excuse was _____ , but Julian remained unconvinced. (plausable, plauzible, plausible)
14. The _____ value of high doses of vitamin C has not been proven. (medicinal, medicenal, medinical)
15. All his life he has carried the _____ of his father's suicide. (stegma, stigna, stigma)

Part III: Each of the core list words in the following sentences either *needs an additional letter* or *has an extra letter.* In either case, correct the spelling.

1. Abigail has already planed her summer vacation.
2. Beulah has a pleassant face but an irritating personality.
3. Cynthia always takes the path of least posible resistance.
4. Deborah has a huge quanity of war cries at her disposal.
5. Edith can acomplish any task she undertakes.
6. Frances charges addmission to all her parties.
7. Gertrude has always been affraid of lightning.
8. Hilda was alowed to carry a reduced program at college.
9. Irma has always been faithful to her relligion.
10. Judy invariably makes a ressponse to any comment she hears.
11. Socrates' mind was never sullied by an inoble thought.
12. Bartholomew is a student of the medievial period in history.
13. Be sure to alocate enough money in the vacation budget to buy souvenirs.
14. As a soap opera character, her life consists of one crissis after another.
15. As with most teenage boys, his housekeeping skills are deplorrable.

Part IV: Proofread the following passage, correcting all errors in spelling.

The minister left the alter for the pulpit. Thoes who thouht he might make a speach of vengance aganst sin did not acurately know their man. "I addmit weakness in myself," he began. "He who alows it in himself must surely allow it in others."

CHAPTER TEN

Prefixes

Prefixes are syllables affixed to the beginnings of words to change their meanings. Prefixes aren't as numerous as roots, but they are important vocabulary building tools. For instance, they combine with root words to generate extensive word families.

Here's a small example: In the last chapter you learned that the Latin root **fac** means "make" or "do." When you attach certain prefixes with that root (or its variants, **fact** and **fect**), you can build innumerable words:

Prefix	Root	Words
af- *(meaning "to")*	**fect**	**affect** *("to do to, to influence")*
bene- *(meaning "good")*	**fact (or)**	**benefactor** *("one who does good")*
ef- *(meaning "from")*	**fect**	**effect** *("result from doing")*
de- *(meaning "to lower")*	**fect**	**defect** *("lack of that which is required in order to complete")*

Prefixes also qualify the meanings of the words to which they are attached. The Latin root **cursor**, for example, means *"runner."* The Latin prefix **pre-** means *"before."* The literal meaning of **precursor** is "something or someone who runs before." In current usage, it means "a forerunner, a sign foretelling what is to come." Another example is the word **anarchy**. The Greek root **arch** means *"government"* or *"leader."* The Greek prefix **an-** means *"not."* **Anarchy** therefore means "without government" or "without a leader."

Several kinds of spelling problems are common in writing words with prefixes. The following rules should help you avoid these prefix pitfalls.

Rule 1: When adding a prefix, don't change the spelling of the original word. Sometimes the last letter in a prefix is the same as the first letter of the root word. In such cases, the correct spelling is a *double letter*. Consider these examples:

dis + solve = di**ss**olve
dis + satisfy = di**ss**atisfy

over + rule = ove**rr**ule
over + reach = ove**rr**each

un + natural = u**nn**atural
un + nerve = u**nn**erve

mis + spell = mi**ss**pell
mis + step = mi**ss**tep

ir + rational = i**rr**ational
ir + regular = i**rr**egular

com + mingle = co**mm**ingle
com + miserate = co**mm**iserate

Occasionally, people become confused in the other direction. They get the idea that the prefix ends in a double letter and misspell words by adding a letter that doesn't belong. However, no prefix ends with double letters—all end in a single consonant or vowel. Here are some common examples of this error:

dis + agree = disagree
    NOT **diss**agree
mis + understand = misunderstand
    NOT **miss**understand

Test your skill with this rule by completing the following exercise.

Exercise 10.1

Circle the correctly spelled choice in each of the following sentences.

1. To many listeners pure jazz sounds like pure [disonance] [dissonance].
2. The hunchback of Notre Dame was [mishapen] [misshapen].
3. Her skiing [mishap] [misshap] laid her up for a week.
4. Sergeant Penn received a deserved [commendation] [comendation] for his bravery.
5. Air and water pollution in the cities [disuaded] [dissuaded] Max from leaving his mountaintop cabin.
6. Lou was deeply [disappointed] [dissappointed] when Sue refused to marry him.
7. The [missprint] [misprint] in the newspaper ad caused a riot at the store.

8. The confused politician once again [mispoke] [misspoke].
9. If you feel so strongly, why not write a letter to the [comissioner] [commissioner]?
10. Jerry is quite [disimilar] [dissimilar] from his brother Ted.

Rule 2: Use the **meaning** of the word to figure out the correct spelling of the prefix. Some prefixes are very similar in pronunciation and in spelling but quite different in meaning. If you memorize the meanings of the following prefixes, you will be able to tell which spelling is correct.

Prefix	Meaning	Words
pre-	before (in place or time)	precede, precipitate
per-	through, throughout	permeate, perspire
pro-	forward, in favor of	promote, procession
di- (dis-, dif-)	away, apart, not	discern, disarm, difficult
de-	lower, reduce	demote, descend
inter-	among, between	interstate, intercept
intra-	within	intrastate, intramural
intro-	inward, to the inside	introvert, introduce
hyper-	above, beyond	hyperbole, hypersensitive
hypo-	under, beneath	hypodermic, hypothesis
ante-	before	antecedent, anteroom
anti-	against	antipathy, antiseptic

Note: Unfortunately, there are exceptions to these spellings that cause much confusion—so be careful. Certain words using the meaning of the prefix **ante-** have adapted their spelling to **anti**—for example:

anticipate—"to feel or realize beforehand"

antipasto—"appetizer served before the meal"

Also be careful with words that *seem* to have one of these prefixes, but actually are derived from completely different historical roots—for example, *antenna* and *antique*.

Before you study the last rule on spelling prefixes, complete the following exercise to test your skill.

Exercise 10.2

Circle the correctly spelled choice in the following sentences.

1. Pronouns must agree with their [anticedents] [antecedents] in number, gender, and person.
2. Why must Eric [presist] [persist] in being so unpleasant?
3. Edwige refused to [divulge] [devulge] the location of her secret files.
4. A good [anteseptic] [antiseptic] will help that wound heal properly.
5. The letter **i** [precedes] [procedes] the letter **j**.
6. If you cannot answer the question, ask your [prefessor] [professor].
7. I know of no [antedote] [antidote] for lovesickness.
8. Just when one [desease] [disease] is irradicated, another is discovered.
9. He gave the police officer a [description] [discription] of the burglar.
10. No matter how grim things look, I shall not [dispair] [despair].

Rule 3: Use the **pronunciation** of the word to figure out the correct spelling of the prefix. Many prefixes have variant spellings to allow for easier pronunciation when they are combined with particular roots. Because our tongues normally seek the easiest way to pronounce any word, these prefixes have been adapted or simplified— either because they are easier to say or because they simply sound right according to the taken-for-granted pronunciation rules in English. For instance, the prefix **com-** (which means "together with") changes to **co-** when combined with **education** to make the word **coeducation**. *Comeducation* just doesn't sound right. And neither does *comlateral*. In this case, **com-** adapts to **col-** to create the word **collateral**. Listed below are the original prefixes and their variants that cause the most frequent spelling problems:

Prefix	Meaning	Words
AD-	to, toward	adhere, advertisement, adjudicate
a-		ascend, ascribe, averse
ac-		accede, accord, accumulate
af-		affect, affix, affiance
ag-		aggravate, aggrandize, aggregate
al-		allot, allude, allocate
an-		annex, announce
ap-		apparent, applaud
ar-		arrive, arraign
as-		assist, assent, assemble, assign
at-		attendance, attest, attenuate

Prefix	Meaning	Words
DIS-	from, away	disturb, disease
di-		divert, digress, diligent
dif-		difference, differ, diffident, diffuse
IN-	in, into, on *(nouns and verbs)*	intrude, invent, into, incline
il-		illuminate, illustrate
im-		import, implore, imbibe
ir-		irrigate, irradiate
IN-	not *(adjectives)*	indecent, informal
il-		illiterate, illegal, illicit
ig-		ignorant, ignoble
im-		immodest, immoral, improper
ir-		irregular, irrational
SUB-	under, beneath, down	submarine, submerge, submit
suc-		succumb, succinct
suf-		suffix, suffer, suffuse
sug-		suggest
sup-		supplant, supplicate, suppress
sus-		suspend, suspect, sustain

Flex your spelling muscles on this rule by working the following exercise before you go on to the Chapter Mastery Test.

Exercise 10.3

Circle the *one* correctly spelled choice in the word groups below. The words in each group all have a variation of the same original prefix.

1. acscribe   admix   astain
2. angrieve   arpendage   allergic
3. dilate   disgress   difract
4. disension   disperse   diffigent
5. irruminate   inprint   impound
6. initial   imjure   ilhibit
7. ilhuman   innoble   irritable
8. impassive   imfamous   iglegal
9. sugculent   susscribe   subversion
10. suffocate   supmit   substain

Most of the prefixes in modern English derive from Old English, Latin, and Greek. The following list includes many of the most commonly used prefixes, their meanings, and a sampling of words that include them. The original language of each prefix is indicated by a capital letter in parentheses — (E) for Old English, (L) for Latin, and (G) for Greek.

There are so many prefixes in English that it is impossible to list all of them, and almost futile to try to learn every one that is listed. However, by learning the most common and trickiest ones—and by using the following list as a reference resource when you are stumped—you'll be able to speak and spell with confidence.

PREFIXES

Prefix	Meaning	Words
A- (G) **(an-)**	not, without	apathetic, atheism, aseptic
A- (E)	at, in, on, to	ahead, asleep, afoot, aground
AB- (L) **(a-, abs-)**	from, away from	abnormal, abduct, absent, avert
AD- (L) **(a-, ac-, af-, ag-, al-, an-, ap, ar-, as-, at-)**	to, toward	adjust, adjacent, adorn, adopt
AMBI- (L)	both	ambivalent, ambiguous
AMPHI- (G)	around, on both sides	amphitheater, amphibious
ANA- (G)	again, up, against	anachronism, analogy, analogue
ANTE- (L)	before	antedate, antecedent
ANTI- (G) **(ant-)**	opposed, against	anticlimax, antidote, antonym
ARCH- (G) **(archi-)**	chief, earliest	architect, archangel
AUTO- (G)	self	autocrat, automobile, autonomy
BE- (E)	throughout, over	bedeck, besiege, besot, bemoan
BE- (E)	by, in	because, beside
BENE- (L)	good, well	beneficial, benevolent
BI- (L) **(bis-)**	two, twice	biped, bicycle, bimonthly, bisect
CATA- (G)	down, downward	cataclysm, catastrophe
CIRCUM- (L)	around	circumstance, circumvent
CON- (L) **(com-, co-, col-, cor-)**	with	congress, correlate, colloquy
CONTRA- (L) **(contro-, counter-)**	against	contradict, controversy, countermand
DE- (L)	from, down	denounce, decapitate, debase
DI- (L) **(dis-, dif-)**	from, away	divert, dismiss, diffuse
DIA- (G)	through, between	dialogue, diagram, diagonal
EC- (G)	from, out of	eccentric, ecstatic, eclectic

Prefix	Meaning	Words
EPI- (G) (**ep-, eph-**)	upon, beside	epidemic, epilogue, ephemeral
EQUI- (L)	equal	equanimity, equilateral
EU- (G)	good, happy, well	euphonious, eulogy, euthanasia
EX- (L)	former	ex-wife, ex-president
EX- (L) (**e-, ef-, ec-**)	out, from, away	exotic, exit, enervate, ecstasy
EXTRA- (L)	outside, beyond	extraordinary, extravagant
FOR- (E)	against, not	forbid, forbear, forlorn
FORE- (E)	before	foretell, foreground, forehead
HETERO- (G)	different	heterogeneous, heterodoxy
HOMO- (G)	same	homogeneous, homosexual
HYPER- (G)	extreme, over	hypersensitive, hyperbole
HYPO- (G)	under, below	hypothesis, hypochondriac
IN- (L) (**il-, im-, ir-**)	in, into, on (*nouns and verbs*)	intrude, imbibe, irrigate
IN- (L) (**il-, im-, ir-, ig-**)	not (*adjectives*)	indecent, illiterate, improper
INFRA- (L)	under, beneath	infrared, infrastructure
INTER- (L)	between, among	interfere, interpose, interurban
INTRA- (L)	inside, within	intravenous, introspect
MAL- (L) (**male-**)	bad	malefactor, malevolent, malformed
META- (G)	after, beyond	metaphysics, metabolism
MIS- (E)	error, defect, wrong	mistake, mislay, misbehave
MULTI- (L)	much, many	multiply, multitude, multicolor
NEO- (G)	new	neophyte, neoclassical, neonatal
NON- (L)	not	nonexistent, nonsense, nonconformist
OB- (L) (**o-, oc-, of-, op-**)	against, out	obstruct, obsolete, occult, offend
OUT- (E)	beyond, completely	outdo, outside, outbreak
PARA- (G)	beside	parallel, paradox, paraphrase
PER- (L)	through, throughout	persist, pertinent, perceive
PERI- (G)	around, about	perimeter, periscope, peripatetic
POLY- (G)	many	polygamy, polysyllabic, polyglot

Prefix	Meaning	Words
POST- (L)	after	postpone, postscript, posterior
PRE- (L)	before	predict, prevent, predecessor
PRO- (L)	forward, in favor of	provoke, propose, proclivity
PRO- (G)	earlier, in front of	prologue, program, proselyte
RE- (L)	again, back	repeat, remind, recall, refulgent
RETRO- (L)	back, backward	retroactive, retrospect, retrograde
SUB- (L)	under, beneath	submarine, supplant, succumb
(**suc-, suf-, sug-, sup-, sus-**)		
SUPER- (L)	above, over	superimpose, superficial, surfeit
(**sur-**)		
SYN- (G)	with, together	synonym, synopsis, symphony
(**sym-, syl-**)		
TRANS- (L)	across, over	transport, transmit, traduce
(**tra-**)		
TRI- (L)	three	triangle, triumvirate
ULTRA- (L)	beyond, extreme	ultramodern, ultraconservative
UN- (E)	not	untie, undo, uninspired
UNDER- (E)	beneath, less than	undertow, underrate, underwrite
UNI- (L)	one	uniform, unilateral, unity
UP- (E)	high	upshot, uplift, upset
WITH- (E)	from, against	withstand, withdraw, withhold

Chapter Mastery Test

Test your mastery of **prefixes** by applying the information you have learned in this chapter to the following spelling situations.

Each of the following sets of words has the same prefix. The meaning of the prefix is given with each set. Complete the words in the space provided.

1. Prefix meaning "good, well"
   _____ volence
   _____ ficiary
   _____ diction
2. Prefix meaning "down, downward"
   _____ pult
   _____ ract

3. Prefix meaning "between, among"
   _____ mediate
   _____ rupt
   _____ cept

4. Prefix meaning "before"
   _____ monition
   _____ text
   _____ serve

5. Prefix meaning "before"
   _____ cast
   _____ boding
   _____ ground

6. Prefix meaning "with"
   _____ cur
   _____ tract
   _____ spire

7. Prefix meaning "above, over"
   _____ mount
   _____ render
   _____ face

8. Prefix meaning "one"
   _____ versal
   _____ que
   _____ son

9. Prefix meaning "out, from, away"
   _____ terior
   _____ tinction
   _____ haust
   _____ cerpt

10. Prefix meaning "equal"
    _____ valent
    _____ nox
    _____ librium

Core Word List #10

accuser	annually	device	irascible	permanent
accuses	anticipate	difficult	later	phase
accusing	apologized	dilemma	loose	prophecy
adolescence	apology	dining	lose	quiet
adolescent	brilliance	disillusioned	mere	scene
all together	brilliant	due	moral	source
already	calendar	except	morale	symbol
altogether	cigarette	hear	morally	where
amount	cite	here	off	whole
annual	correlate	ingenious	peace	whose

Core Word Mastery Test

Master the spelling of these words from the core list and learn their meanings before you try to learn those in the chapters ahead. **Remember:** *In spelling, your goal is a perfect score.*

Part I: Circle the appropriate word choices in the sentences below. Note that although in some instances all the choices are correctly spelled, only one is appropriate *in context*.

1. Hush! Twilight has just fallen and all is [all ready] [already] [quite] [quiet].
2. [All together] [Altogether] there were six of us harmoniously working [all together] [altogether].
3. I am unable to [site] [cite] for you a single [devise] [device] that will make all your decisions.
4. The train was [do] [due] at six o'clock and would have arrived, [accept] [except] that it was derailed.
5. Now [here] [hear] this, all of you gathered [hear] [here] before me.
6. When his diabolically [ingenious] [ingenuous] plan failed, the mad scientist began at once a method that he felt would work at a [later] [latter] time.
7. I was at a [loss] [loose] to explain his [loss] [loose] moral code.
8. Does a low [moral] [morale] standard improve [morale] [moral] or lower it?
9. Can a prophet [prophesy] [prophecy] [piece] [peace], or is a [prophecy] [prophesy] of that kind merely guesswork?
10. The [whole] [hole] [seen] [scene], was a shambles after the bomb exploded.

Part II: Match the core list word in *Column B* with the appropriate context in *Column A*. If the core list word is misspelled, correct it.

Column A

1. I am no longer enchanted.
2. I expect that to happen.
3. The flag means more than a bit of cloth.
4. He says that I stole the money.
5. Check that date.
6. It happens every year.
7. He is not yet an adult.
8. I don't know what to do.
9. It will last forever.
10. I'm sorry.

Column B
a. symbal
b. accusser
c. adolesent
d. anual
e. anticipate
f. appology
g. pernament
h. calander
i. dillema
j. disillusioned

Part III: Each of the core list words in the following sentences needs an *additional* letter to make it correct. Add the necessary letter.

1. His errant acts make him moraly suspect.
2. When a wife acuses her husband of bad faith, he had better have a ready answer.

3. Adolesence is one of the most painful but exciting periods of life.
4. Annualy, at the end of each year, the company issues its financial report.
5. The pianist gave a briliant performance of Mozart's concerto.
6. May I have a cigarete?
7. How can one corelate vocabulary with intelligence?
8. I find learning spelling rules not as dificicult as I had expected.
9. I fell of the pier into the water.
10. I have asked repeatedly whos book this is.

Part IV: Proofread the following passage, correcting all spelling errors.

Having concluded his latest fase—accussing his friends of faithlessness—Gerard appologised, explaining that he never knew wher the sourse of his moods was. An, furthermore, he added, a man of his brillance ought not be held accountable for mear rudeness, whether in discussing the ammount of a bill or the character of the guests assembled at the dinning table. Everyone simply concluded that Gerard was basically irrascible.

CHAPTER ELEVEN

Suffixes

Like prefixes, suffixes are syllables affixed to a root word to change its meaning. Suffixes typically don't change the meaning of a word as drastically as prefixes do—they *enhance* or *adjust* the meaning. However, they do more than simply change meaning. They also change the word's *grammatical function*—its *part of speech*. The following lists provide a handy guide to the suffixes corresponding to different parts of speech.

Noun Suffixes

A. Abstract Nouns: These suffixes signify *"state of," "act of,"* or *"quality of."*

Suffix	Words
-AL	committal, approval
-ACY	celibacy, democracy
-AGE	bondage, salvage, marriage
-ANCE	severance, dilligence,
(**-ancy, -ence, -ency**)	emergency
-ATION	civilization, union, dissension
(**-tion, -ion, -sion**)	
-CE (**-cy**)	independence, piquancy
-DOM	freedom, kingdom, serfdom
-HOOD	boyhood, manhood, falsehood
-ICE	avarice, cowardice
-ISM	communism, baptism
-MENT	government, statement, agreement
-NESS	happiness, lewdness, deafness
-SE	defense, offense, pretense
-SHIP	partnership, penmanship
-TH	warmth, depth, length
-TY (**-ity**)	security, modesty, femininity

B. Concrete Nouns: These suffixes signify *"one who does," "one who is."*

Suffix	Words
-AN (-ant, -ent)	partisan, participant, vagrant, student
-ARD (-art, -ary)	drunkard, braggart, notary
-EE (-eer, -ess)	legatee, auctioneer, tigress
-ER (-ar, -ier, -or)	laborer, scholar, clothier, auditor
-IC (-ist, -ite, -yte)	cynic, sadist, Brooklynite, acolyte
-LING	yearling, foundling

Adjective Suffixes

A. These suffixes signify *"resembling," "full of," "belonging to," "degree."*

Suffix	Words
-AC (-al, -an, -ar, -ary)	cardiac, seasonal, Russian, circular
-AL	parental, coincidental
-ED	fated, crippled, intended
-FOLD	tenfold, manifold
-FUL	spiteful, vengeful, joyful
-IC (-ical)	anemic, inimical, nomadic, maniacal
-ISH	foolish, English, childish
-IVE	restive, furtive, secretive
-ORY (-ary)	admonitory, hortatory, voluntary
-IOUS (-ous)	gracious, efficacious, spacious
-MOST	foremost, hindmost, inmost
-ULENT	succulent, fraudulent
-WARD	wayward, northward
-Y	funny, creepy, bony, greedy

B. These suffixes signify *"capable," "able to."*

Suffix	Words
-ABLE	movable, curable, peaceable
-IBLE	irresistible, visible
-ILE	fertile, ductile, puerile
-IVE	conclusive, adaptive, coercive

Verb Suffixes

These suffixes signify *"to make."*

Suffix	Words
-ATE	procreate, animate, perpetuate
-EN	moisten, deepen, quicken
-FY	qualify, fortify, stupefy
-IZE (-ise)	magnetize, criticize, sterilize

Adverb Suffixes

These suffixes signify *"in the manner of," "in the direction of."*

Suffix	Words
-LY	meagerly, evenly, closely
-WARD	inward, outward, toward
-WISE	crosswise, otherwise

Consider the different ways you can use suffixes to change words from one part of speech to another:

From Verbs to Abstract Nouns: Add **-tion, -ion, -sion, -ation, -al, -se, -ment, -ance**

compile	compilation
compel	compulsion
refuse	refusal
govern	government
confer	conference
transpose	transposition
expend	expense
buoy	buoyance

From Verbs to Concrete Nouns: Add **-er, -or, -ant, -ent**

audit	auditor
expedite	expedient
labor	laborer
supply	supplicant

From Adjectives to Abstract Nouns: Add **-ness, -ity, -ce, -cy**

happy	happiness
romantic	romance
loquacious	loquacity
dependent	dependency

From Nouns to Verbs: Add **-ize**

terror	terrorize
economy	economize
drama	dramatize
anesthesia	anesthetize

From Adjectives to Verbs: Add **-ize, -en, -fy**

fertile	fertilize
thick	thicken
liquid	liquefy
solid	solidify

From Nouns to Adjectives: Add **-ful, -less, -ious, -ous, -y, -al, -ic, -ish, -an, -ary, -ed**

hope	hopeful
chill	chilly
nature	natural
psychosis	psychotic
America	American
end	endless
beauty	beauteous
fever	feverish
imagination	imaginary
trust	trusted

From Verbs to Adjectives: Add **-able, -ible, -ive**

reverse	reversible
manage	manageable
evade	evasive
repair	reparable

From Adjectives to Adverbs: Add **-ly, -wise**

handy	handily
angry	angrily
length	lengthwise
excitable	excitably
false	falsely
like	likewise

Now that you've got an idea of the flexibility and usefulness of suffixes, let's look at some of the typical trouble spots we come across when trying to spell them.

-ABLE or -IBLE

Both of these suffixes serve as endings for adjectives, both have the same meaning ("capable, able to"), and both sound the same. Obviously, they present a serious problem for spellers. Here are some tips to help you master **-able/-ible**.

Rule 1: If the noun form of the word ends in **-ation**, then the adjective form will end in **-able**. Here are some examples:

admir**ation**	admir**able**
dur**ation**	dur**able**
imagin**ation**	imagin**able**
separ**ation**	separ**able**

Rule 2: If the noun form ends in **-ition, -tion, -sion,** or **-ion,** then the adjective form will end in **-ible**. Here are some examples:

admis**sion**	admis**sible**
corrup**tion**	corrupt**ible**
collec**tion**	collect**ible**
reduc**tion**	reduc**ible**

Note: Many words that fall under this rule have a **double s** preceding the **-ible** suffix—like **admissible**. Use the **double s** as another useful spelling clue. Here are some examples:

permi**ssion**	permi**ssible**
transmi**ssion**	transmi**ssible**

There's one common exception to this rule that you should memorize—**predictable**. Unlike the other examples here, the noun form is **prediction**.

Rule 3: If the root is a **complete word** (or lacks only a final e), the suffix is usually **-able**. Note the following examples:

detest	detest**able**
credit	credit**able**
excite	excit**able**
size	siz**able**

Rule 4: If the root is not a **complete word**—in other words, if it cannot stand alone—the suffix is usually **-ible**. Look at these examples:

poss**ible**	irresist**ible**
elig**ible**	terr**ible**
aud**ible**	horr**ible**
plaus**ible**	respons**ible**
vis**ible**	invinc**ible**

Rule 5: If the root ends in the sound of **hard c** (as in **cat**) or **hard g** (as in **good**), the suffix is probably **-able**. Study the examples below:

despi**cable**   navi**gable**
expli**cable**   dele**gable**

Rule 6: If the root ends in the sound of **soft c** (as in **cellar**) or **soft g** (as in **gem**), the suffix is probably **-ible**. These words are more common than those having the sound of hard **c** or hard **g**. Look at these examples:

redu**cible**   incorri**gible**
for**cible**   le**gible**
iras**cible**   eli**gible**

One last point you should remember when facing the **-able/-ible** dilemma: **-able** occurs *four times more often* than **-ible**. If you can't figure out which spelling is correct according to the rules above, use **-able** and you're 75 percent likely to be right.

Before we cover the other spelling rules in this chapter, let's test your skill with the rules governing **-able** and **-ible**.

Exercise 11.1

In the space provided, add the appropriate suffix—either **-able** or **-ible**—to the incomplete words in the following sentences.

1. With the aid of modern medicine, leprosy is now a cur_____ disease.
2. To experience true fulfillment, people must value the intang_____ as well as the material things in life.

3. Might Moe stood forth as the invinc_____ conqueror of the entire block.
4. Roscoe's drunken behavior at the funeral was deplor_____.
5. His arguments are rarely plaus_____.
6. Old Wilbur Tiddle, as irasc_____ as ever, still runs the general store.
7. Can you provide me with demonstr_____ proof of your theory?
8. Despite June's whining, her mother remained immov_____.
9. His voice was so low it was nearly inaud_____.
10. Many constellations are vis_____ on clear nights.

ANT/-ENT and -ANCE/ENCE

-Ant and **-ent** serve as endings for either *nouns* or *adjectives*. Both suffixes have the same meaning—"an agent" (*noun*) and "a quality" (*adjective*). **-Ance/-ence** serve as endings only for *nouns*. Again, both suffixes have the same meaning—"action, state, quality." Like **-able** and **-ible**, these suffixes sound alike and are a knotty problem for most spellers. Here are a few guidelines to help you untangle the knots.

Rule 1: If the verb form of the word has an **a** in the last syllable, then the suffix will be **-ant** or **-ance**. Here are some examples:

radi**ate**	radi**ant**,	radi**ance**
hesit**ate**	hesit**ant**,	hesit**ance**
toler**ate**	toler**ant**	toler**ance**
domin**ate**	domin**ant**,	domin**ance**

Rule 2: If the verb form of the word is **accented on the final syllable** and ends with **-er**, then the suffix will be **-ent** or **-ence**. Typically in these cases, the **-ent** suffix requires a suffix of its own: **-ial**. Look at these examples:

refer	referential,	reference
prefer	preferential,	preference
defer	deferential,	deference

Rule 3: If the root ends in the sound of **soft c** (as in **cellar**) or **soft g** (as in **gem**), the suffix is probably **-ent** or **-ence**. Study these examples:

innocent,	innocence
magnificent,	magnificence
intelligent,	intelligence
negligent,	negligence

Keep in mind that root words ending in **hard c** or **hard g** are rare. A few examples:

significant,	significance
extravagant,	extravagance

Rule 4: If the root ends in **-sist** or **-xist**, the suffix is probably **-ent** or **-ence**. Here are some examples:

exist	existent,	existence
insist	insistent,	insistence
consist	consistent,	consistence
persist	persistent,	persistence

Unfortunately, these four rules don't cover most of the spelling situations involving **-ant/-ance** and **-ent/ence**. Your best bet is to memorize the most common words with these suffixes. Many of these words have been included in your core word lists.

However, here's a sampler for you to work with.

-ANT/-ANCE
abundant, abundance
brilliant, brilliance
elegant, elegance
entrant, entrance
ignorant, ignorance
important, importance
irrelevant, irrelevance
observant, observance
repentant, repentance
significant, significance
tolerant, tolerance

-ENT/-ENCE
absent, absence
abstinent, abstinence
adherent, adherence
coherent, coherence
confident, confidence
consequent, consequence
competent, competence
convenient, convenience
dependent, dependence
diffident, diffidence
diligent, diligence
divergent, divergence
eminent, eminence
impertinent, impertinence
imprudent, imprudence
indulgent, indulgence
insolent, insolence
magnificent, magnificence
patient, patience
permanent, permanence
prominent, prominence
provident, providence
reverent, reverence
resident, residence
violent, violence

Note: Only a few words end with the sound-alike **-ense**. You can avoid spelling errors by memorizing them: def**ense**, exp**ense**, imm**ense**, off**ense**, pret**ense**, susp**ense**.

Test your skill with **-ant/-ance** and **-ent/-ence** before you study the other troublesome suffixes in this chapter.

Exercise 11.2

In the space provided, add the appropriate suffix—either **-ant/-ance** or **-ent/-ence**—to the incomplete words in the following sentences.

1. Adolesc_____ is a stage of development that begins at twelve and sometimes ends.
2. She thinks $5,000 a month is barely sufficient for subsist_____ .
3. The commandant would stand for no interfer_____ from the prisoners.
4. Jonas is a remarkably persist_____ fellow.
5. He wasn't merely ignor_____ , he was mean tempered as well.
6. For Martha, simply taking a bubble bath was an extravag_____ .
7. I am toler_____ of all, except those I hate!
8. Why are you hesit_____ about accepting his offer?
9. The librarian will help you locate the refer_____ book you need.
10. Her insist_____ finally broke his resist_____ .

-AL, -EL, or -LE

The suffix **-al** is attached to adjectives and nouns to signify "of, belonging to, appropriate to." Study these examples.

Words Ending in **-AL**

annu**al**	person**al**
arriv**al**	propos**al**
brut**al**	recit**al**
classic**al**	riv**al**
deni**al**	roy**al**
fat**al**	sign**al**
logic**al**	trivi**al**
magic**al**	

The endings **-el** and **-le** are not suffixes. They are simply known as *affixes*. Many words end in **-le**, but the **-el** ending is much less common than either **-al** or **-le**. Learn the common words in this list to avoid getting mixed up.

Words Ending in **-EL**

bush**el**	nov**el**
canc**el**	nick**el**
chann**el**	pan**el**
flann**el**	parc**el**
funn**el**	quarr**el**
jew**el**	satch**el**
kenn**el**	shov**el**
kern**el**	swiv**el**
mod**el**	trav**el**
mors**el**	trow**el**

-LY or -ALLY

Adverbs ending in **l** add the suffix **-ly**—except for those which end in **double l**, which simply add a **-y**. Here are some examples:

accidental**ly**	hopeful**ly**
especial**ly**	skillful**ly**
final**ly**	truthful**ly**
natural**ly**	dul**ly**

Add **-ally** only when the adverb ends in **-ic**:

> automatic**ally**   emphatic**ally**
> basic**ally**   mathematic**ally**

Review your skill with **-al/-el/-le** and **-ly/-ally** before going on with the remainder of this chapter.

Exercise 11.3

Circle the correctly spelled choice in the sentences below.

1. David [accidently] [accidentally] washed his white slacks with his red T-shirt.
2. The dictator ruled his country with [brutal] [brutel] power.
3. Her [clericle] [clerical] skills leave quite a bit to be desired.
4. I can see a [kernal] [kernel] of truth in what you are saying.
5. Dr. Lee told her [truthfally] [truthfully] that she had only forty years to live.
6. The president didn't think much of Ambrose's [proposel] [proposal].
7. The old gal just doesn't have much [sizzel] [sizzle] anymore.
8. Although he speaks [logically] [logicly], he behaves quite differently.
9. Fox used a mere pawn to deliver the [fatel] [fatal] blow to his chess opponent.
10. I would like to send this [parcal] [parcel] by air mail.

The remaining troublesome suffixes follow no spelling rules. Mastery of these mischief-makers depends upon remembering which spelling is most common and learning the most frequently used words that have alternate spellings.

-ER, -OR, or -AR

Most concrete nouns end in **-or** rather than **-er** or **-ar**. Study the lists below to familiarize yourself with common words that have **-er** and **-ar** suffixes.

Concrete Nouns Ending in **-ER**

advertis**er**	offic**er**
beginn**er**	passeng**er**
bookkeep**er**	prison**er**
consum**er**	publish**er**
employ**er**	purchas**er**
farm**er**	push**er**
foreign**er**	receiv**er**
interpret**er**	shopp**er**
labor**er**	stenograph**er**
manag**er**	teach**er**
manufactur**er**	tell**er**
own**er**	writ**er**

Concrete Nouns Ending in **-AR**

begg**ar**	registr**ar**
li**ar**	exempl**ar**

Other Common Words Ending in **-AR**

calend**ar**	peculi**ar**
coll**ar**	regul**ar**
doll**ar**	simil**ar**
famili**ar**	singul**ar**

-ISE, -IZE, or -YZE

Most verbs using this suffix end in **-ize**. Look over the following lists to get a sense of the words that end in **-ise** and **-yze**.

Common Verbs Ending in **-ISE**

advert**ise**	franch**ise**
adv**ise**	merchand**ise**
ar**ise**	rev**ise**
chast**ise**	superv**ise**
comprom**ise**	surm**ise**
desp**ise**	surpr**ise**
disgu**ise**	repr**ise**

Other Common Words Ending in **-ISE**

demi**se**
enterpr**ise**

Verbs Ending in **-YZE**

anal**yze**
paral**yze**

-ARY or -ERY

Of the more than 300 words with the **-ary/-ery** suffix, the majority use the **-ary** spelling. Only two commonly used words end in **-ery**:

cemetery
stationery ("writing materials")

-EFY or -IFY

Almost all verbs using this suffix end with an **-ify** spelling. Here are the most common exceptions using the **-efy** ending:

lique**fy**
rare**fy**

Test your skill with these troublesome suffixes before you attempt the Chapter Mastery test.

Exercise 11.4

Circle the spelled choice in the following sentences.

1. The sergeant [chastized] [chastised] Ruth for the speck of dust on her boots.
2. Forgive us our debts as we forgive our [debters] [debtors].
3. This new lotion can [beautify] [beautefy] even my dog's complexion.
4. I can [criticize] [criticise] my own work, but don't you try it!
5. At the Bargain Basement Warehouse, the [consumor] [consumer] is king!
6. Raquel noticed a smudge of red lipstick on Derrick's shirt [coller] [collar].
7. Will John [testefy] [testify] against his mother?
8. Skippy decided to ask his [employar] [employer] for a salary increase.
9. The intense heat of an atomic reaction can [liquify] [liquefy] everything in the vicinity.
10. Are you a participant or just a [spectater] [spectator] of life?

Chapter Mastery Test

Test your mastery of **suffixes** by applying the skills and information you have learned in this chapter to the following spelling situations.

Part I: In the space provided, write the correct combination of root and suffix for each of the following words.

	Root	Suffix	Combination
1.	human	-ize or ise?	_____
2.	element	-ary or -ery?	_____
3.	acquaint	-ence or -ance?	_____
4.	indicat	-er or -or?	_____
5.	digest	-able or -ible?	_____
6.	profession	-ally or -ly?	_____
7.	swiv	-el or -le?	_____
8.	calend	-ar or -or?	_____
9.	indulg	-ance or -ence?	_____
10.	commend	-ible or -able?	_____
11.	refus	-al or el?	_____
12.	descend	-ent or -ant?	_____
13.	comprom	-ize or -ise?	_____
14.	cemet	-ary or -ery?	_____
15.	cynic	-ally or -ly?	_____
16.	antagon	-yze or -ize?	_____
17.	elig	-ible or -able?	_____
18.	susp	-ence or -ense?	_____
19.	infirm	-ery or -ary?	_____
20.	radiat	-er or -or?	_____

Part II: Circle the *one* correctly spelled choice in the following groups of words.

1.	spectater	peculiar	conveniance
2.	symbolize	coronery	persistant
3.	destructable	riddle	reverant
4.	solitery	nickle	impertinent
5.	remembrence	perishable	acquittel
6.	squabble	interpretor	detestible
7.	permanant	honorary	paralize
8.	elegence	normle	permissible
9.	sponsor	neutralise	tributery
10.	exercize	discipal	abstinent

Core Word List #11

absence	advertiser	competition	escape	literature
abundance	advertising	dealt	especially	maybe
abundant	advertisement	dissatisfied	every	medicine
acclaim	another	divide	genius	plausible
accustom	apparatus	divine	hopeless	politician
actual	appreciate	dropped	hoping	practice
actuality	area	during	huge	presence
actually	cemetery	easily	hundred	safety
adequate	children	eighth	idea	sentence
adequately	competitor	entertainment	laid	themselves

Core Word Mastery Test

Master the spelling of these words from the core list and learn their meanings before you try to learn those in the chapters ahead. **Remember:** *In spelling, your goal is a perfect score.*

Part I: Match the core list word in *Column B* with the appropriate context in *Column A*. If the core list word is misspelled, correct it.

Column A

1. We have plenty of everything.
2. He deserves our applause.
3. That will be satisfactory.
4. Bury the dead.
5. Get them to buy our product.
6. Beat the other fellow.
7. His talent is extraordinary.
8. It's enormous.
9. How many years make a century?
10. Will this device work?

Column B

a. apparetus
b. hunderd
c. abundence
d. advertissing
e. aclaim
f. adequate
g. hugge
h. compitition
i. cemetary
j. genuis

Part II: One letter in each of the core list words in the sentences below is incorrect. Substitute the correct letter.

1. Absense makes the heart grow fonder.
2. An abundent harvest will make the farmers happy.
3. He performs his tasks adaquately.
4. Send your material to the advertisor and he will write the copy.
5. I appresiate your efforts in my behalf.
6. We must find a way to outsell our competetor.
7. A house must not devide against itself.

8. Prisoners rarely excape from their cells.
9. I fail to get your idear.
10. The druggist will send the medecine to your home shortly.

Part III: Circle the one correctly spelled choice in the sentences below.

1. I cannot [acustom] [accustom] myself to her face.
2. Did he [actually] [actualy] arrive on time?
3. I placed an [advertizement] [advertisement] in the newspaper.
4. Ask the [childeren] [children] to eat in their own room.
5. I am [hopeing] [hoping] that you will be our guest for tea.
6. We are quite [disatisfied] [dissatisfied] with our room service.
7. Your red hat is an [especally] [especially] attractive one.
8. The study of [litrature] [literature] is arduous but rewarding.

9. In the [presence] [presense] of his neighbors, he kissed his wife.
10. We live on the [eigth] [eighth] floor.

Part IV: Proofread the following passages, correcting all errors in spelling.

1. To succeed, a musical comedy must provide entertaiment. Durring the show the actors must seem to enjoy themselfs; they must deliver lines to one annother easely and naturally; every moment must suggest that this play is the finished product of months of actul practise and rehearsal. Mebbe then the play will flourish even if the soprano's voice is not devine.

2. The pollitician in my araea is a plausable fellow of high presance. He has dropped mighty words about public safty and layed several cornerstones. But in actuallity he has delt with no significant issue; he has, in brief, proved himself to be a hopless incompetent.

PUNCTUATING WORDS

CHAPTER TWELVE

The Hyphen

When most people think of punctuation marks, they think of commas, question marks, colons, dashes, and other "signals" that indicate relationships between parts of sentences and even between sentences. Some people also may think of quotation marks and parentheses, which are punctuation marks as well. But many people don't think of **hyphens** and **apostrophes**—punctuation marks for *words* rather than phrases, clauses, and sentences. However, many troublesome spelling errors result from not knowing how to use these specialized tools. This chapter and the next provide you with the information you need to avoid these errors.

The **hyphen [-]** is used both to *divide* words and to *combine* them. Let's take a look at the rules governing both of these uses.

Dividing Words

As a divider, the hyphen is used to break a word into syllables, usually at the end of a line of writing. Most people *hyphenate* words when writing or typing to avoid having one line that is much shorter or longer than those before and after it. One basic rule guides all hyphenation, with several smaller rules outlining how to apply the basic rule in different situations:

Rule 1: Divide words between syllables. Usually you can identify the break between syllables by pronunciation. For instance, say these words aloud as you note where the hyphen is placed.

tire-some	pro-mote	hack-ney
mid-get	ab-surd	pat-ent
our-selves	func-tion	gar-ment

Rule 2: Divide words of more than two syllables into meaningful units. You should still break the word into syllables, but choose the dividing point that will most help the reader understand the word easily. Look at these examples of better and worse hyphenation:

Better	Worse
depart-ment	de-partment
happi-ness	hap-piness
per-secute	perse-cute
imita-tion	imi-tation

Rule 3: When two consonants stand together between two vowels, divide between the consonants. Look at these examples:

pas-sion	moun-tain
mil-lion	struc-ture
run-ning	pas-ture

Rule 4: Never divide one-syllable words. Most one-syllable words obviously "look wrong" when hyphenated, but others are a little trickier to spot. Look at these examples:

Correct	Incorrect
wrong	wr-ong
breadth	bre-adth
climbed	clim-bed
change	chan-ge
spelled	spel-led

Rule 5: Never divide on a syllable with a silent vowel. Study these examples:

Correct	Incorrect
passed	pass-ed
helped	help-ed
people	peo-ple
tailor	tai-lor

Rule 6: Never divide a word after a single letter—and, when possible, avoid creating two-letter syllables. Here are examples of both types of errors:

One-letter syllable
  abroad NOT a-broad
  enough NOT e-nough
  alone NOT a-lone
  among NOT a-mong

Two-letter syllable
  until NOT un-til
  stricken NOT strick-en
  only NOT on-ly
  heaven NOT heav-en

Complete this exercise to test your skill at **dividing** words.

Exercise 12.1

In the space provided, hyphenate the words that can be *divided correctly*. For words that should *not* be hyphenated, write "okay" in the space.

1. buoyant   _____
2. broached   _____
3. eventually   _____
4. changing   _____
5. country   _____
6. losses   _____
7. onus   _____
8. criticism   _____
9. amen   _____
10. noisy   _____

Combining Words

The rules regarding word combination are a little more complicated than those regarding word division. As a combiner, the hyphen is used most often to join separate words together into a new unit of meaning—a *compound*. There are compound nouns, compound verbs, and compound adjectives. In certain situations hyphens also are used to attach *prefixes* to nouns, verbs, and adjectives.

As two words become regularly associated, the hyphen is used to link them together. Eventually, most compound words are fused into a single word, without the hyphen as a connecting device. Here are some examples of familiar compound words that originally were hyphenated and now are fused:

basketball	classroom
swaybacked	bookkeeper
trademark	freestanding
stopover	moonrise

Because the hyphen is a transitional mark, it is used inconsistently. The following rules will serve you in most situations. However, your best bet is to consult a current dictionary when in doubt.

Rule 1: Use the hyphen when a noun is combined with another word or words to form a new noun. A noun can be combined with another noun—as in **light-year** or **secretary-treasurer**—or with other parts of speech—as in **double-talk** (adjective) or **Johnny-on-the-spot** (prepositional phrase). Other examples of noun compounds are:

great-aunt	left-winger
fighter-bomber	president-elect
owner-manager	belt-tightening
attorney-at-law	bell-bottoms

Rule 2: Use the hyphen when a verb is combined with another part of speech to form a noun. Verbs can be combined with objects or with prepositions to create new nouns. Consider these examples:

trade-in	know-nothing
shake-up	cure-all
come-on	has-been

Rule 3: Use the hyphen when a verb must be modified by a noun, adjective, or preposition in order to convey the intended meaning. Here are some examples:

double-park	breast-feed
carbon-date	Indian-wrestle

Rule 4: Use the hyphen when two or more words are used as a single adjective **preceding** a noun—**only** when there is a possibility of misreading. Note the many different word combinations that might fall under this rule:

- Noun/Noun: **father-son** act, **bomb-squad** commander
- Adjective/Noun: **high-class** waitress, **no-fault** insurance
- Noun/Participle: **moth-eaten** sweater, **life-giving** operation
- Adjective/Participle: **foul-smelling** garbage, **foreign-born** citizen
- Adverb/Participle: **well-known** author, **far-reaching** plan
- Verb(s)/Conjunction: **hit-and-run** accident, **do-or-die** attitude
- Phrases: **out-of-date** idea, **blow-by-blow** description
- Numbers: **twenty-first** birthday, **ten-year** ban

Remember: In the many cases where the meaning is clear without the hyphen, omit it. For example:

- **Don't** use a hyphen with most adverb/adjective combinations. **Never** hyphenate if the adverb ends in **-ly**:

  Incorrect: highly-trusted employee
  Correct: highly trusted employee
  Incorrect: very-beautiful woman
  Correct: very beautiful woman
  Incorrect: most-famous celebrity
  Correct: most famous celebrity

- **Don't** use a hyphen with adjective-adjective or adjective-noun combinations when chances of misreading are negligible:

  Incorrect: light-green sweater
  Correct: light green sweater
  Incorrect: high-school diploma
  Correct: high school diploma
  Incorrect: Red-Cross workers
  Correct: Red Cross workers

Rule 5: Use hyphens to attach the prefixes **ex-**, **all-**, and **self-**. Here are some common examples:

ex-champion	all-purpose	self-reliant
ex-wife	all-knowing	self-starter
ex-president	all-star	self-hate

Rule 6: Use hyphens to combine two or more proper adjectives and to attach prefixes to proper nouns or proper adjectives. Note these examples:

Anglo-Saxon	anti-Semitic
Franco-American	mid-Atlantic
Sino-Russian	pre-Christian

Rule 7: Use hyphens to combine letters and words. Here are some examples:

x-axis	U-boat
U-turn	B-sharp

Rule 8: Use hyphens for clarity. Hyphens are always permissible to prevent confusion. In some cases, without the hyphen the word would be mistaken for another with identical spelling—for instance:

recover: I haven't yet **recovered** from the accident.
re-cover: I haven't yet **re-covered** the chair.

In other cases, the hyphen is sometimes necessary to avoid putting too many vowels or consonants together—for instance:

shell-like	anti-inflammatory
grass-seed	semi-indirect
co-edition	re-engineered

However, consult your dictionary. Many words with double vowels or consonants, such as **reenact** and **snaillike**, are now one word.

Rule 9: Use the hyphen for words and phrases your dictionary lists as hyphenated. These words may or may not fall into the above categories. When in doubt, your dictionary is your best guide.

See how well you can do at **combining** words before you attempt the Chapter Mastery Test.

Exercise 12.2

In the space provided, hyphenate the words below that can be *combined correctly.* For words that should *not* be hyphenated, write "okay" in the space.

1. a well preserved corpse _____
2. the light blue dress _____
3. feeling self assured _____
4. the jack in the box _____
5. the kindest hearted man _____
6. a wait and see attitude _____
7. the North American companies _____
8. the anti China rally _____
9. the old family album _____
10. the co owner of the store _____

Chapter Mastery Test

Review the spelling rules you have learned in this chapter covering the use of **hyphens**. Then complete the following questions to test your mastery of these spelling skills.

Part I: In the space provided, hyphenate the words below that can be *divided correctly.* For words that should *not* be hyphenated, write "okay" in the space.

1. unite _____
2. muffin _____
3. often _____
4. passage _____
5. dwindling _____
6. idol _____
7. vexed _____
8. about _____
9. sizzling _____
10. excessive _____

Part II: In the following sentences circle the words that should be combined with a hyphen.

1. The victorious opposition leader pledged that his government would adopt a pro United States middle road government.
2. The most heavily traveled section of the new turnpike will soon have extra lighting in order to cut down on nighttime accidents.
3. An all night session left the legislators weary, knee deep in unfinished business, and still lacking the two thirds majority to defeat the bill.
4. The New Air all cargo transport planes offer dependable, on time deliveries to eighty six countries and territories on all six continents.

5. In the final play off at Wimbledon, first ranked Boris Becker soundly defeated his archrival Ivan Lendl, who was less than pleased to be runner up.
6. The President elect announced today that his father in law had reemerged from retirement in order to take over as his right hand man.
7. When the A bomb was first tested, ex President Truman expressed concern for the far reaching effects of nuclear fission on our one and only planet.
8. Gun toting members of a right wing gang did a shakedown of all the town's least respectable citizens in mid December, just in time for the holiday season.
9. I wore my homely cousin's hand me downs all my growing up years, although my nimble fingered mother managed to make them look brand new.
10. My Scotch Irish grandmother married a Native American Indian, which makes me one quarter Cherokee and one eighth Irish.

Core Word List #12

admirable	dissonance	illiterate	mysterious	sleigh
aggrandize	divulge	illusion	mystery	slew
agreeable	elicit	imbibe	panicked	sovereign
buoyant	expatriate	immovable	peaceable	stationery
chastise	facetious	irrigate	persistent	straight
civilian	fiend	kissable	picnicking	tier
climactic	fierce	liquefy	priestly	transient
college	fiery	mien	reducible	virtuoso
collegiate	glacier	mishap	skein	waxen
digress	gratuitous	misshapen	slain	wield

Core Word Mastery Test

Master the spelling of these words from the core list and learn their meanings before you try to learn those in the chapters ahead. **Remember:** *In spelling your goal is a perfect score.*

Part I: Each of the core list words in the following sentences either *needs an additional letter* or *has an extra letter.* In either case, correct the spelling.

1. Comic Red Skelton could always ellicit a smile from my grouchy uncle.
2. Dorothy went on a glacer skiing expedition last summer.
3. That mishapen Christmas package was wrapped by our three-year-old.
4. This summer heat can liqueffy an ice cream cone in less than thirty seconds.

5. His high level of body fat makes him boyant in the water.
6. When two beliefs contradict one another, we experience cognitive disonance.
7. Mabel operates under the ilusion that she'll be discovered in the corner drugstore like Lana Turner.
8. The climmactic moment of the ceremony was when the groom said, "I don't know."
9. With this drought, the farmers will be forced to irigate.
10. Money is the sovreign lord to whom he pledges his loyalty.
11. Arriving at boot camp, Frankie said a sad good-bye to civillian life.
12. The drunken expatrate drank rum in the tropical shade and remembered the good old days.
13. She's so casual she uses paper towels for stationnery.
14. When I realized my purse was missing, I paniked.
15. Their colegiate years were the best of their lives.

Part II: One word in each of the following sentences has a blank space for *one* letter. If a letter should be added to make the spelling correct, add it. If the word is correct as is, ignore the blank space and leave the word as is.

1. At this late date, your concern is gratu_____tous.
2. The professor would di_____gress at the slightest invitation.
3. Getting a flat tire was only the *first* mis_____hap of the evening.
4. Caught in traffic, the resourceful youngsters were picnic_____ing in the back of their pickup truck.
5. I promise I will never divul_____ge your secret.
6. The Quakers are a peac_____able folk.
7. The foul f_____iend from Fresno finally floated in formaldehyde.
8. Bunyon gives to charity solely in order to a_____grandize himself.
9. Jerome looks priest_____ly in his black nightshirt.
10. Her whereabouts are a myst_____ry to everyone.

Part III: Circle the *one* correctly spelled choice in each of the following sentences.

1. Mary has many [admirible] [admirable] qualities, but generosity isn't one of them.
2. Police say the victim was [slain] [slein] in his sleep.
3. The side effects of the medication are unpleasant but [transient] [transeint].
4. Spoiled young children learn early how to [wield] [weild] power.
5. I can't decide whether to go to a trade school or a community [collage] [college].
6. Her brand of humor depends upon irony and [facetious] [facitious] remarks.
7. When William comes home from school, I will [chastize] [chastise] him for breaking the window.

8. Judith's [mysterous] [mysterious] behavior has the whole office buzzing.
9. He has trapped himself in a twisted [skein] [skien] of lies.
10. Our whole argument is [reducible] [reducable] to this: You're wrong!
11. I see him now! He's sitting on the first row in the second [tier] [teir] of seats.
12. At his peak, Craig could [inbibe] [imbibe] eighteen cream sodas in one afternoon.
13. Have you ever actually heard [sliegh] [sleigh] bells jingle?
14. Frieda claims to be [iliterate] [illiterate] with computers.
15. Bozo displays a [feirce] [fierce] loyalty to his master.

Part IV: Proofread the following paragraph, correcting all spelling errors.

When the passionate young Romero first saw the lovely mein of Lulu, cupid's arrow flew strait to his pounding heart. She sluw him with her feiry eyes. He proclaimed to have never met with such kissible lips. But although Romero was persistant and agreeible, Lulu was imovvable. She was a vertuoso of the cold shoulder and the waxxen expression.

CHAPTER THIRTEEN

The Apostrophe

Apostrophes are used to form **contractions**, to indicate **possession**, and in a few cases, to form **plurals**. This chapter will help you master contractions and possessives. The use of apostrophes to form plurals was covered in **Chapter 4: Plurals and Tenses**.

Contraction

The chief problem in spelling with apostrophes results from confusing *contracted* forms with *possessive* forms. In contractions the apostrophe is used to show a *mechanical* relationship between words and letters. But in possessives the apostrophe is used to show a *grammatical* relationship between ideas.

With contractions the apostrophe is used to indicate that one or more letters have been left out of a word. Just remember—**put the apostrophe exactly where the original letter or letters would be**. Study these examples:

Original Word(s)	Contraction
I am	I**'m**
he will	he**'ll**
she is	she**'s**
they are	they**'re**
are not	aren**'t**
does not	doesn**'t**
cannot	can**'t**
should have	should**'ve** [NOT should **of**]
would have	would**'ve** [NOT would **of**]
who is	who**'s**

Sometimes words are contracted for poetic purposes or to indicate dialect—for example:

over - o'er   Angels watch o'er us as we sleep.
just - jus'   I jus' wanna go fishin'.

Possession

With possessives the apostrophe is used—*usually* along with the letter **s**—to indicate **ownership**, **origin**, or **measurement**. Here are a few examples:

> Robert's car
> the judge's decision
> a week's vacation

Because most words add **'s** to form the possessive, it is simpler to learn the exceptions. Study each of the rules below to get a handle on correct spelling of possessives.

○ **Add only the apostrophe if a plural common noun ends in -s**—for example:

writers' conference   monkeys' tricks
Negroes' rights   hostesses' gowns
boys' games   uncles' jokes

○ **Add the 's if a proper noun ends in -s**—for example:

Dickens's novels   Youmans's followers
Mr. Hastings's butler Arkansas's capital

But Jesus, Moses, and Greek names of more than one syllable ending in **-es**, such as Euripides, don't require the extra **s** after the apostrophe.

○ **Add the 's to only the second of two persons who share possession**—for instance:

> Art and Sofia's baby
> the director and assistant director's report

○ **Add the 's to only the last word in a compound noun**—for example:

> his father-in-law's money
> the attorney general's office

○ **Never use apostrophes to show possession with personal or relative pronouns.** These pronouns have special possessive forms. Here are some examples:

his book	the book is **hers**
our music	the music is **theirs**
its house	**whose** house?

○ **Apostrophes can be used to form the possessive of nouns that stand for inanimate objects—especially when they are part of an idiomatic expression.** In many cases, however, it's better to write the phrase differently. Study these examples:

Acceptable	Better
the wild's call	the call of the wild
the book's pages	the pages of the book
logic's principles	principles of logic
money's evils	evils of money

The following examples are idiomatic expressions that are best written as possessives:

wit's end	sun's rays
duty's call	earth's surface
hair's breadth	razor's edge

Chapter Mastery Test

Review the spelling rules you have learned in this chapter covering the uses of the **apostrophe**. Then complete the following questions to test your mastery of these spelling skills.

Part I: In the space provided, correctly spell the **contracted** form of the following clauses.

1. you will see   _____
2. they are here   _____
3. here is to health   _____
4. nobody is home   _____
5. they are not sure   _____
6. I should have gone   _____
7. who is going   _____
8. we cannot stay   _____
9. he does not drive   _____
10. who could have
    known   _____

Part II: In the space provided, correctly spell the **possessive** form of the following phrases.

1. the gowns of the
   princesses   _____
2. the novels of
   Twain   _____
3. the home of Mar-
   gie and Jeff   _____
4. the healing of a
   month   _____
5. the agreement of
   gentlemen   _____
6. the rise of the
   river   _____
7. the opinion of the
   lieutenant colonel   _____
8. the leashes of the
   dogs   _____
9. the legacy of the
   Bauhaus   _____
10. the end of the day   _____

Core Word List #13

ashen	erotic	ingenuous	pier	sizzling
averse	erratic	intangible	predictable	sobriety
chateau	extravagant	interference	proffering	species
chocolate	gaiety	invincible	qualify	subsistence
competent	guardian	martial	receipt	supplant
despair	heinous	munificent	reference	surfeit
diffident	hierarchy	neighbor	reprieve	systematic
dwindling	ignite	omniscient	serviceable	usable
efficacious	infallible	opulent	sheik	vein
embargo	inference	patient	shriek	visible

Core Word Mastery Test

This is the final Core Word Mastery Test. Do not proceed to the Final Test of Core List Words until you have taken this test. Some of the words from this mastery test may appear on that review test. Once more, **Remember:** *In spelling your goal is a perfect score.*

Part I: Circle the correct word choices in each of the following sentences.

1. While Dr. Bones is certainly [competent] [compatent], he isn't necessarily [infalible] [infallible].
2. That was a decade of [gaity] [gaiety] for the owners of the [chateau] [chataeu].
3. Your kisses [ignite] [ingite] an [errotic] [erotic] flame under my toes.
4. Big Steve heard about the [embarggo] [embargo] when he reported for work down at [Peir] [Pier] 42.
5. Her [extravegant] [extravagant] shopping habits resulted in a [surfeit] [surfiet] of shoes.
6. Love may be [intangible] [intangable], but it nevertheless is [visable] [visible].
7. All [species] [speices] are organized into a [heriarchy] [hierarchy] from the simplest creatures to the most complex.
8. My fear of causing a car accident is [guardien] [guardian] of my [soberiety] [sobriety] when I am driving.
9. She is so consistently [eratic] [erratic] that she's almost [predictible] [predictable].

10. The brassy energy of the [marital] [martial] music convinced the soldiers that they were [invincible] [invinsible].

Part II: One of the core words in each of the following sentences needs an *extra* letter to make it correct. Add the necessary letter.

1. Suzie can't decide whether she likes chocolat or vanilla better.
2. You must bring in the sales receit if you want to return a garment.
3. When she was a child, Veronica believed her father was omniscent.
4. Mr. Smith was so ingenous when he went to Washington that Congress didn't know what to make of him.
5. Has that unscrupulous hussy suplanted me in your heart?
6. Suddenly a piercing shiek broke the silence.
7. This arrangement is servicable, if not truly desirable.
8. His dwinling popularity drove the senator to drink.
9. Miss Lucy is difident with strangers.
10. I'm sick and tired of your interfrence in my affairs!

Part III: Proofread the following passage, correcting all errors in spelling.

1. My neigbor was in such dispair from the advers circumstances of his life that he cut his viens with a razor. His

face was so ashin I though he might die, but Fate gave him a repreave. He is currently a patent at the state mental hospital.

2. The desert sun was sizling down on the shiek's shabby tent. By infrence, one might conclude he was living a susistence existence, but such was not the case. The shiek was a munnificant desert lord who lived in opalence.

3. A refrance book is only as efficasious as it is useable. However, a systamatic study of most texts profering this kind of assistance shows that few qualafy. It's a henious crime against scholarship!

PART FIVE

SPECIALIZING IN SPECIAL TERMS

CHAPTER FOURTEEN

Business and Law

The words below are frequently used in business and law—in correspondence, reports, contracts, and the like. Often they are misspelled. Master their spelling; then test your knowledge of their *spelling* and *meanings* in the exercises that follow.

abandonment (uh-BAN-dun-ment)
accessory (ak-SES-ur-ee)
accountant (uh-KOWNT-unt)
acknowledgment (ak-NAHL-edj-ment)
adjudicate (ad-JU-dee-kayt)
affidavit (af-u-DAY-vit)
alibi (AL-i-by)
alimony (AL-i-moh-nee)
annul (a-NUL)
arraign (u-RAYN)
auditor (AU-di-tur)

bailiff (BAY-lif)
bankrupt (BANK-rupt)
bigamy (BIG-ah-mee)
burglary (BUR-glah-ree)
coercion (coh-UR-shun)
collateral (co-LAT-er-ul)
counselor-at-law (COWN-sel-ur)
coupon (KOO-pon)
defendant (di-FEN-dunt)
dunning (DUN-ing)
embezzle (em-BEZ-ul)
entrepreneur (on-tre-pru-NEWR)
franchise (FRAN-chyz)
homicide (HOM-i-syd)
indictment (in-DYT-ment)
ledger (LEJ-ur)
liability (ly-uh-BIL-i-tee)
liquidate (LIK-wuh-dayt)
management (MAN-ij-ment)

merchandise (MER-chun-dyz)
mortgage (MOR-gij)
negotiable (ni-GOH-shi-uh-buhl)
personnel (per-suh-NEL)
promissory (PROM-uh-sohr-ee)
subpoena (suh-PEE-nuh)
syndicate (SIN-duh-kit)
tariff (TAYR-if)
usury (YEW-zhuh-ree)
writ (WRIT)

Chapter Mastery Test

Complete the sentences below by choosing the appropriate word from the following list. If any words in the list are incorrectly spelled, correct them.

A.   frandchise   managment
         tarrif   merchandize
         ledger   colatteral
         embezzeled   personnal
         negotiable   auditer

1. A high _____ on imported watches raises their price on the American market.
2. Recent purchases of _____ are entered on the _____ .
3. The _____ of the soda water company issued a _____ to two bottling companies, giving them permission to use the company's label.
4. The _____ , when he examined the company's books, discovered that $10,000 had been _____ .
5. How much _____ must I offer to procure the loan?

6. After you sign this check, it will become _____ .
7. The _____ manager interviewed six candidates for the position of floorwalker.

B.   coupons   duning
         acountant   promisery
         liabillity   liquidate
         morgage   enterprener
         acknowledgement sindicate

1. When Jones failed to pay his _____ note, his creditor sent him strong _____ letters.
2. An efficient _____ makes his credit and debit ledgers balance.
3. My favorite pastime is clipping stock _____ and estimating their value.
4. Our _____ pooled its finances and invested in government bonds.
5. A man who underwrites the expense of a business is known as an _____ .
6. Although I wrote to the bank inquiring about a second _____ on my house, I have received no _____ from them.
7. To raise money to pay debts, the company was compelled to _____ its surplus stock.

C.   accessary   bigimy
         annull   allimoney
         abandonment   alibbi
         burglery   inditement
         coercion   defendent

1. Because he was accused of _____ , the defendant agreed to _____ all but one of his several marriages.
2. When a husband deserts his wife, the law terms his act _____ , and his wife may sue for _____ .

3. Having helped the thief to escape, his sister was arrested as an _____ after the fact.
4. The accused _____ had a plausible _____ .
5. The state prosecutor sought to obtain an _____ against the man charged with _____ .
6. Police officers are not permitted to use _____ to force a confession from a prisoner.

D.

afidavitt	bankrup
writt	subpoena
councilor-at-law	ajudicate
araign	baillif
homicide	usury

1. Lacking funds or property with which to pay his debts, the _____ businessman filed an _____ notifying his creditors of his situation.
2. The judge issued a _____ , a court order that the _____ found harmful to his client's rights.
3. The witness received a _____ ordering him to testify in court.
4. The disputants asked the judge to _____ their differences.
5. The _____ escorted the accused murderer to the judge's bench, where the judge began to _____ the prisoner on charges of _____ .
6. One who charges illegal interest rates for loans is guilty of _____ .

CHAPTER FIFTEEN

Health and Medicine

The words below are frequently used in biological science and medicine—in articles and books. Master their spelling; then test your knowledge of the *spelling* and *meanings* in the exercises that follow.

adenoids (AD-uh-noyd)
allergy (AL-ur-gee)
amphibian (am-FIB-ee-un)
anatomy (uh-NAT-uh-mee)
antibiotics (an-ti-by-OT-ik)
antihistamine (an-ti-HIS-tuh-meen)
antiseptic (an-ti-SEP-tik)
antitoxin (an-ti-TOK-sin)
astigmatism (uh-STIG-mah-tiz-um)
bacilli (ba-SIL-y)
barbiturate (bahr-BITCH-uh-rayt)
botany (BOT-uh-nee)

carbohydrate (kahr-boh-HY-drayt)
cardiology (kahr-DEE-awl-uh-jee)
carnivorous (kahr-NIV-uh-rus)
catarrh (kuh-TAWR)
chlorophyll (KLOHR-uh-fil)
chromosome (KRO-muh-sohm)
diagnosis (dy-uhg-NOH-sis)
eczema (EK-suh-muh)
embryo (EM-bree-oh)
epilepsy (EP-uh-lep-see)
evolution (ev-uh-LOO-shun)
fungus (FUNG-us)
hemorrhage (HEM-uh-rij)
heredity (hi-RED-uh-tee)
hormone (HOHR-mohn)
hypertension (hy-pur-TEN-shun)
inoculate (i-nok-yuh-layt)
instinct (IN-stingkt)

laryngitis (lar-un-JI-tis)
mammal (MAM-uhl)
microscope (MY-kruh-skohp)
obstetrics (uhb-STET-riks)
organism (OHR-guh-niz-um)
paralysis (puh-RAL-uh-sis)
parasite (PAR-uh-syt)
pediatrician (pee-dee-uh-TRISH-un)
penicillin (pen-uh-SIL-in)
protoplasm (PROH-tuh-plaz-um)
streptomycin (strep-toh-MY-sin)
vaccine (VAK-seen)
vertebrate (VUR-tuh-brayt)
virus (VY-rus)
zoology (zoh-OL-uh-jee)

Chapter Mastery Test

Complete the sentences below, choosing the appropriate word from the following list. If any word in the list is incorrectly spelled, correct it.

A.
streptimycin	pencillin
barbitchurate	antihistimine
highpertension	zology
amphibbian	fungus
embrio	bottany

1. To ease the stress of _____ , doctors occasionally recommend a _____ to sedate a patient's nerves.
2. Three of the most recent "wonder" drugs are _____ , _____ , and _____ .
3. A turtle, because it lives on either land or sea, is known as an _____ .
4. In the science of _____ , one may encounter the _____ of an ape, whereas in _____ , one is more likely to examine _____ and other forms of plant life.

B.
mammel	carniverous
vertebrate	parisite
evilution	heredety
instinkt	annatomy
microscope	organizm

1. The wolf, a _____ animal, prefers chickens for its diet rather than daisies.
2. Whales have backbones and milk glands. Like us, they are _____ s and _____ s.
3. In the _____ of life from its primitive stages, all forms of nature have been afflicted with _____ s.
4. By looking into a powerful _____ , you can study a living _____ too small to be seen with the naked eye.
5. Certain parts of our _____ , such as our facial characteristics, height, and the like, are the result of our _____ .
6. Responses that we cannot control—hunger, fear, thirst—we attribute to _____ .

C.
bacili	carbohydrate
clorophil	chromocom
protoplasim	laryngitis
addenoids	catarr
anteseptic	alergy

1. _____ may color your plants green, but it cannot make goats smell sweet.
2. Bacteria that cause disease are known as _____ .
3. Unless a plant contains _____ , the essential matter of all life, it cannot produce the starchy substance known as _____ .
4. Each _____ contains genes, the elements that determine our hereditary traits.
5. _____ is an inflammation of the mucous membrane of the nose.

6. A speaker whose _____ have swelled may sound as if he has _____ .
7. People who suffer from an _____ to pollen or dust should live in _____ rooms.

D.

antibioticks	virus
vacine	dignosis
obstetricks	hemorage
antitocksin	pediatrisian
ekzeema	horemon

1. Dr. Jones believes that the only good _____ is a dead one that has been converted into a _____ to prevent disease.
2. _____ are substances capable of destroying bacteria.
3. After the doctor's _____ revealed that she was pregnant, Mrs. Brown began to read articles about _____ .
4. A _____ is more likely to treat a baby

effectively than a podiatrist.

5. Injections of _____ extract often help to ease the skin irritation caused by _____ .
6. A _____ will combat disease, but it cannot prevent _____ of blood vessels.

E.

cardiology	astigmitizm
innoculate	paralysis
epelipsy	

1. If you have _____ , you need glasses to reform the blurred images you now see.
2. Patients with heart ailments are treated by specialists in _____ .
3. To _____ one with the Salk vaccine practically assures immunity from infantile _____ .
4. _____ is known also as falling sickness.

CHAPTER SIXTEEN

Science and Technology

The words below are frequently used in science and technology—in articles about physics and mathematics. Study them and test your knowledge and skill in the Chapter Mastery Test.

abacus (AB-uh-kus)
amplifier (AM-pluh-fy-er)
angle (ANG-gul)
cathode ray (KATH-ohd ray)
circumference (suhr-KUM-fuhr-uhns)
cosmic ray (KOZ-mik)
cyclotron (SY-kluh-tron)
decimal (DES-uh-mul)
denominator (di-NOM-uh-nay-tur)

electronics (i-lek-TRON-iks)
fidelity (fy-DEL-uh-tee)
fissionable (FISH-un-uh-bull)
frequency modulation (FREE-kwun-see moj-uh-LAY-shun)
hypotenuse (hy-POT-uh-noos)
infinity (in-FIN-uh-tee)
integer (IN-tuh-jur)
isosceles (y-SOS-uh-leez)
jet propulsion (JET pruh-PUL-shun)
nuclear fission (NYOO-kli-ur FISH-un)
numerator (NYOO-muh-ray-tur)
perpendicular (pur-pun-DIK-yuh-lur)
quotient (KWOH-shunt)
supersonic (soo-pur-SON-ik)

Chapter Mastery Test

Complete the sentences below by choosing the appropriate word from the following list. If any word in the list is incorrectly spelled, correct it.

A.

fidellity	cathode ray
cycletron	amplifeir
nooclear fishon	infinnity
suppersonic	electronics
abbacus	cosmick rays

1. A more popular expression for _____ is "splitting the atom."
2. A _____ can produce atomic projectiles whose energy exceeds a hundred million volts.
3. A sensitive _____ improves the _____ of recorded music.
4. Television images are made up of electrons beamed by a _____ .
5. _____ enter our atmosphere from outer space.
6. _____ aircraft travel at 738 mph, exceeding the speed of sound.
7. An _____ would be of little help in computing sums ranging up to _____ .
8. _____ is the branch of physics that studies the characteristics of electrons.

B.

decimal	demonator
quoteint	numerator
integer	angel
circumferance	hypotenoose
isosceles	perpandiculer

1. A whole number is an _____ ; any tenth part of a whole number is a _____ .
2. When writing fractions, place the _____ above the line, the _____ below the line.
3. The number obtained when one quantity is divided by another is a _____ .
4. Is it simpler to find the _____ of a circle or the _____ of an _____ triangle?
5. The side of a right-angled triangle opposite the right angle is called the _____ .
6. A man standing erect is _____ to the floor on which he stands.

C.

jet propellsion	fissionible
frequency	modulaition

1. Rocket aircraft, operated by _____ , achieve speeds beyond that of sound.
2. Hydrogen bombs are constructed of _____ materials that explode with incredible force.
3. _____ , better known as FM, produces clearer radio reception than AM reception.

CHAPTER SEVENTEEN

Engineering and Architecture

The words below are frequently used in articles and books about engineering and architecture. Study them and test your knowledge and skill in the Chapter Mastery Test.

abutment (uh-BUT-ment)
baroque (buh-ROHK)
buttress (BUT-ris)
Byzantine (BIZ-un-teen)
cantilever (KAN-tuh-leev-ur)
colonnade (kol-uh-NAYD)
cornice (KOR-nis)

corridor (KOR-uh-dur)
facade (fuh-SAHD)
gargoyle (GAHR-goyl)
girder (GUR-dur)
Gothic (GOTH-ik)
lancet (LAN-sit)
mosaic (moh-ZAY-ik)
nave (NAYV)
Romanesque (ROH-muh-nesk)
rotunda (roh-TUN-duh)
trellis (TREL-is)
veneer (vuh-NEER)
wainscot (WAYN-skot)

Chapter Mastery Test

Complete the sentences below by choosing the appropriate word from the following list. If any word in the list is incorrectly spelled, correct it.

A.

barokue	Gothic
Romanesk	gargoils
faceade	lancet
knave	abuttments
rotunder	girder

1. The _____ of a _____ building is usually flamboyant.
2. _____ cathedrals generally have towering spires, symbolic of man's spiritual aspirations.
3. The semidarkness of a _____ abbey reflects the austerity of the monastic spirit.
4. Those fantastic animals projecting from building gutters are known as _____ .
5. Arch bridges are supported by _____ .
6. Skyscrapers use the _____ as their skeletal structure.
7. _____ windows allow light to fall upon the aisles and _____ of a cathedral.

8. The entrance hall of the Capitol in Washington, D.C., is known as a _____ .

B.

moseaic	Byzanteen
colonades	corridor
butteresses	trellus
venear	wainscott
cornise	cantilever

1. _____ architecture is characterized by elaborate decoration.
2. The Parthenon in Greece has an exquisite arrangement of _____ around the outer portion of the building.
3. The walls of the church are supported by _____ , which lean against it.
4. The floor of the entrance _____ to the mansion was made of inlaid _____ representing the birth of Venus.
5. The walls of the study were finished in _____ , made of thin mahogany _____ .
6. The vines grew wild on the cross strips of the garden _____ .
7. The _____ was elaborately decorated with wreaths and garlands; the rest of the wall was plain.
8. Terraces and bridges can both be supported by _____ s.

CHAPTER EIGHTEEN

Psychology and Religion

The words below are frequently used in psychology and religion—in articles, reports, and books. Often these words are misspelled. Master their spelling; then test your knowledge of their *spelling* and *meanings* in the test that follows.

amnesia (am-NEE-zhuh)
anxiety (ang-ZY-u-tee)
aptitude (AP-ti-tood)
atheism (AY-thee-izm)
baptism (BAP-tizm)
Bible (BY-bul)
blasphemy (BLAS-fuh-mee)
Buddhism (BOOD-izm)
catechism (CAT-uh-kizm)
Christianity (kris-tee-AN-uh-tee)
claustrophobia (klahs-troh-FOH-bee-uh)

congregation (kon-gri-GAY-shun)
crucifixion (kroos-uh-FIK-shun)
deity (DEE-uh-tee)
disciple (di-SY-pul)
empirical (em-PIR-uh-cul)
existentialism (eg-zis-TEN-shul-izm)
extrasensory (eks-truh-SEN-sohr-ee)
gospel (GOS-pul)
hysteria (hy-STEER-ee-uh)
inhibition (in-uh-BI-shun)
intelligence (in-TEL-i-juns)
Judaism (JOO-du-izm)
Mohammedanism (moh-HAHM-med-uh-nizm)
neurosis (nyoo-ROH-sis)
Oedipus complex (ED-uh-pus COM-pleks)
orthodox (or-thoh-DOKS)
parable (PAR-uh-bul)
paranoid (PAR-uh-noyd)

parochial (puh-RO-kee-ul)
prophet (PRAH-fet)
psychiatry (sy-KY-uh-tree)
psychoanalysis (sy-koh-an-AL-u-sis)
psychosis (sy-KOH-sis)
psychosomatic (sy-koh-suh-MAT-ik)
rapport (ruh-POHR)
repression (ri-PRESH-un)
sacrilegious (sak-ri-LI-jus)
senility (sen-IL-u-tee)
sublimation (sub-li-MAY-shun)
theology (thee-OL-uh-gee)
transference (trans-FUR-ens)

Chapter Mastery Test

Complete the sentences below by choosing the appropriate word from the following list. If any word in the list is incorrectly spelled, correct it.

A.   Odepuss complex   pshychoanalysis
       psychiatry   transferance
       anxiety   amnisia
       repression   clauserophobia
       hystaria   senility

1. Fear, apprehension, and foreboding afflict one suffering from _____ .
2. In _____ , Freud's method of treating personality disorders is more rigid than that employed in _____ .
3. A patient suffering from an _____ may, at the stage of therapy known as _____ , shift his feelings of hostility from a parent to his analyst.
4. Prolonged _____ of conscious impulses and desires may on occasion erupt in an acute nervous disorder known as _____ .

5. The victim of _____ fears enclosed spaces; the victim of _____ forgets who he is.
6. The young need not fear _____; even the old, if they remain young in heart, need not fear it.

B.   paranoid   psychosis
       nurosis   inhibisions
       pshychosometic   sublimeation
       inteligence   aptitude
       empirical   rapaport

1. Indigestion, ulcers, and related ailments may often be _____ in origin, the body manifesting the disturbance in the mind.
2. _____ personalities suffer from delusions of persecution, grandeur, and the like.
3. A certain number of _____ can profitably be tolerated by any person, but too many frustrated desires may cause trouble.
4. A mild mental disturbance is a _____ ; a severe one is a _____ .
5. Psychology, an _____ science, bases its conclusions on observation and experiment.
6. Tests designed to predict vocational skills are known as _____ tests; those designed to measure a stage of mental development are known as _____ tests.
7. By _____ , the analyst seeks to redirect antisocial urges into socially acceptable ones.
8. Analysts strive to achieve _____ with their patients, a sense of common interest and feeling that makes the patient trust his analyst.

C.   Bibble   Buddism
       Judyism   Christainity
       Mohammedenism   diety
       athiesm   sacreligious
       orthodox   blasphimy

1. Followers of both _____ and _____ rely upon the _____ as their principal religious text.
2. _____ , a religion of the Far East, is more mystical than _____ , a religion of the Near East.
3. The _____ man of faith regards the disrespectful, _____ expressions of _____ as unforgivable examples of _____ against the _____ .

D.   baptizm   catichesim
       gospel   theologgy
       parocheal   congrigation
       disiple   crucifiction
       prophits   parrable

1. In the New Testament, _____ really means "good news".
2. In Christianity, the principals of faith are taught by _____ , a rigorous method of question and answer.

3. Purification by water immersion is known as _____ .
4. Schools of _____ are staffed by instructors who have had intensive training in _____ subjects, such as religious ethics, religious literature, and religious history.
5. _____ as a method of execution was not new in Jesus' time.
6. The _____ of Israel frequently spoke to their _____s by means of _____s, simple stories with religious and moral significance.
7. Each _____ of Jesus had a particular mission to accomplish.

E.   extrasensery   existentielism

1. _____ has gained followers in the United States as well as in France, where its proponents insist that man alone is responsible for what he is.
2. Certain schools of psychology insist that many of our perceptions should be explained as _____ , rather than as dependent upon what the senses experience.

The Arts: Art, Music, Dance, Literature

The words below are frequently used in the arts, such as art, music, and dance—in newspaper reviews, articles, and literary works. Often they are misspelled. Master their spelling; then test your knowledge of the *spelling* and *meanings* in the Mastery Test that follows.

a cappella (AH-cuh-PEL-uh)
abstraction (ab-STRAK-shun)
arabesque (ayr-uh-BESK)
atonality (ay-tohn-OWL-uh-tee)
autobiography (aw-toh-by-OG-ruh-fee)
ballet (bal-AY)
bibliography (BIB-lee-og-ruh-fee)
cadence (KAY-duns)
ceramic (sur-AM-ik)
chiaroscuro (ki-ahr-uh-SKYEW-oh)
choreography (kor-ee-OG-ruh-fee)

classicism (KLAS-u-sizm)
comedy (KOM-uh-dee)
counterpoint (COWN-ter-poynt)
dissonance (DIS-uh-nuns)
drama (DRAH-muh)
entrechat (ahn-truh-SHAH)
essay (ES-ay)
fugue (FYOOG)
gouache (GWAHSH)
imagery (IM-uj-ree)
lyric (LEER-ik)
madrigal (MAD-ri-gul)
meter (metre) (MEE-tur)
narrative (NAR-uh-tiv)
novel (NOV-ul)
picaresque (pik-uh-RESK)
pirouette (PEER-ew-et)
prologue (PRO-log)
realism (REEL-ism)

rhapsody (RAP-suh-dee)
rhyme (RYM)
rhythm (RITH-um)
romanticism (roh-MAN-tuh-sizm)
satire (SA-tyr)
soliloquy (suh-LI-loh-kwee)
staccato (stuh-CAH-toh)
surrealism (sur-EEL-izm)
symphony (SIM-fuh-nee)
tragedy (TRAJ-uh-dee)

Chapter Mastery Test

Complete the sentences below by choosing the appropriate word from the following list. If any word in the list is incorrectly spelled, correct it.

A.
arebesque	balet
choreography	entrechatte
pihouette	chirascuro
abstraction	ceramick
surealism	guoache

1. Lovers of _____ —the union of dance, mime, and music—attend most carefully to _____ , the arrangement of steps in dance movement.
2. The _____ keeps the dancer on one toe; and the _____ on one foot; and the _____ off the ground altogether.
3. In art, _____ avoids photographic accuracy or any form of outward reality.
4. _____ uses symbols and psychic association as the core for its painting.
5. The technique of painting with opaque watercolors is known as _____ .
6. The distribution of light and dark in a painting is known as _____ .

7. _____ art uses clay and other earth materials to shape exquisite decorative forms.

B.
synphony	madragal
fuggue	rapsody
counterpoint	a capella
attonality	cadense
disonnance	stacatto

1. Bach's D-Minor _____ relies on _____ to achieve its concise symmetry.
2. The _____ usually employs secular themes, whereas the motet—also a choral work—uses sacred themes.
3. Above all else, a _____ should develop a theme during its four movements.
4. The appeal of a _____ is akin to that of free verse—both have the freshness of improvisation.
5. Composers who ignore the conventional tones of music strive for _____ ; often they merely achieve _____ .
6. Unaccompanied choral singing—originally performed in chapels—is called _____ .
7. When the score calls for a transition from a flowing _____ to _____ , the conductor's arms will make short, rapid motions to indicate the beat.

C.
essey	novil
autobiography	tradegy
comedy	sattire
reelism	romanticism
naturelism	classisim

1. While the aging statesman writes his _____ , eager biographers impatiently await his death.
2. Our decade continues to prefer the narrative form of the _____ to the expository form of the _____ .
3. In _____ , characters come to a happy end; in _____ , to an unhappy one.
4. _____ , by portraying the actual and typical, reacted against the invention and imaginative excess of _____ .
5. _____ , closer to realism than to romanticism, often reveals a bias toward pessimism.
6. Reason, restraint, simplicity, and balance are central to the great writings of _____ .
7. To wound, to ridicule, to parody— these are some of the purposes of _____ .

D.   **drama**   **narattive**
         piceresque   **bibliography**

         sololoquy   **imagry**
         ryhthm   **ryhme**
         liric   **prologue**

1. Before preparing a _____ of English _____ , list the names of playwrights whose works are to be included.
2. In the _____ novel, the roguish hero wanders abroad so frequently that the _____ seems to have no central thread.
3. To give a _____ , an actor must assume that no one is listening to him as he speaks aloud his private thoughts.
4. As a poem, the _____ represents an outburst of emotion rather than a narrative.
5. Metaphor and simile are the most conventional figures of poetic _____ .
6. Before the curtain rose, the actor recited the _____ . Its lines were swift in _____ , but they did not _____ .

CHAPTER TWENTY

Foreign Words and Phrases

The words and phrases below are frequently used in business, law, logic, politics, and the arts. Following each word is its language of origin, its pronunciation, and its meaning. Master their spelling; then test your knowledge of their *spelling* and *meanings* in the exercises that follow.

à la carte [French] (ah la KAHRT); dish by dish, with a stated price for each

a priori [Latin] (AH pri-OH-ree); known beforehand

ad infinitum [Latin] (AD in-fi-NY-tum); without limit

alma mater [Latin] (AHL-ma MAH-ter); fostering mother; hence, one's school

anno Domini [Latin] (AN-oh DOM-i-nee); in the year of the Christian era

au revoir [French] (oh re-VWAHR); good-bye till we meet again

auf Wiedersehen [German] (owf VEE-der-Zayn); till we meet again

à la mode [French] (ah la MOHD); (1) dessert served with ice cream; (2) stewed or braised with vegetables and served with gravy; (3) fashionable

bas-relief [French] (bah-re-LEEF); sculpture in low relief

baton [French] (ba-TON); conductor's stick; staff of office

belles lettres [French] (bel LET'r); aesthetic, rather than informational, literature

blitzkrieg [German] (blits-KREEG); a swift, sudden effort or attack

bon vivant [French] (bawn vee-VAHN); lover of good living

bona fide [Latin] (BOH-na FY-de); in good faith

bourgeoisie [French] (boor-zhwah-ZEE); members of the middle class

camouflage [French] (KAM-uh-flahzh); disguise of a camp, and so any disguise expedient

carpe diem [Latin] (KAHR-pe DEE-em); seize the day

carte blanche [French] (KAHRT BLAHNSH); unconditional power

cause célèbre [French] (kohz se-LEB'r); legal case of great interest

connoisseur [French] (kon-i-SUR); one competent as a critic of art

corps [French] (KOHR, *not* KAWRPS); body of persons under common direction

corpus delicti [Latin] (KAWR-pus di-LIK-ty); in a murder case, the victim's body

cortège [French] (kawr-TEZH); procession; train of attendants

coup de grace [French] (KEW de GRAHS); a finishing stoke

crèche [French] (KRESH); representation of the figures at Bethlehem

cuisine [French] (kwe-ZEEN); style of cooking

cul-de-sac [French] (KUL de sak); a blind alley or deadlock

de facto [Latin] (DEE FAK-toh); actually, in fact

détente [French] (day-TAHNT); a relaxation of tensions, as between nations

debut [French] (DAY-byoo, de-BYOO); entrance on a career or into society

debutante [French] (deb-yoo-TAHNT, DEB-yoo-tant); one making a debut

en route [French] (ahn ROOT); on the way

entrée [French] (AHN-tray); (1) main course of a meal, (2) the dish before the main course, (3) right of entry

ersatz [German] (er-ZAHTS); substitute, artificial

ex officio [Latin] (EKS o-FISH-ee-oh); by virtue of an office

ex post facto [Latin] (EKS POHST FAK-toh); done afterward but retroactive

extempore [Latin] (eks-TEM-po-ree); without preparation

facade [French] (fa-SAHD); face of a building, front of anything

faux pas [French] (foh PAH, *plur.* PAHZ); false step; offense against social convention

finis [Latin] (FI-nis); the end

garçon [French] (gahr-SAWN); waiter, boy

gauche [French] (GOHSH); awkward

gourmand [French] (GEWR-mand, gewr-MAHN); a lover of good eating

gourmet [French] (GEWR-may, gewr-MAY); one who shows taste in appreciating good food

gratis [Latin] (GRAT-is); for nothing

hors d'oeuvre [French] (awr DURV); appetizer

in absentia [Latin] (IN ab-SEN-she-a); in absence

in extremis [Latin] (IN eks-TREE-mis); near death

in toto [Latin] (IN TOH-toh); entirely

incognito [Italian] (in-kog-NEE-toh, in-KOG-ni-tow); disguised or concealed

joie de vivre [French] (zhwa de VEE-vr); keen enjoyment of life

laissez-faire [French] (LES-ay FAYR); noninterference

leitmotiv [German] (LYT-moh-teef); theme associated with a person or idea

mal de mer [French] (mal duh MER); seasickness

nom de plume [French] (NOM duh ploom); pen name

non sequitur [Latin] (NON SEK-wi-tur); a conclusion that does not follow from the premises

per diem [Latin] (PUR DY-em); by the day.

persona non grata [Latin] (pur-SOH-na

NON [NAHN] GRA-ta); an unacceptable person

pièce de résistance [French] (pee-ES-duh-ray-zees-TAHNS); main dish; something outstanding

pro rata [Latin] (PROH RAY-ta); according to share

protégé [French] (PROH-te-shay); one under protection of another

savoir faire [French] (SAV-wahr FAYR); social ease and grace

status quo [Latin] (STAT-us KWOH); the state existing

tête-à-tête [French] (tet-a-TET, tayt-a-TAYT); conversation for two alone

tour de force [French] (tewr duh FAWRS); feat of strength or skill

verbatim [Latin] (vur-BAY-tum); word for word

verboten [German] (fer-BOH-ten); forbidden

vis-à-vis [French] (vee-za-VEE); face-to-face

vox populi [Latin] (VOKS POP-yoo-ly); voice of the people

weltanschauung [German] (VELT-ahn-show-ung); worldview

zeitgeist [German] (TSYT-gyst); spirit of the times.

Chapter Mastery Test

Complete the sentences below by choosing the appropriate word from the following list. If any word in the list is incorrectly spelled, correct it.

A.

in ruote	saviore fiar
datehnt	gacon
enteree	in ecstreamus
bone veevent	foxx purpuli
coorpse	statues qwo

perrsuma nun grate	coop de grass
joy di viever	liasezze fiar

1. The _____ was fired after he tripped and spilled the _____ all over a customer as he was _____ to the table.
2. As the young soldier lay _____ , the gray-headed captain of his _____ considered ending the boy's suffering with a swift _____ .
3. The handsome _____ was well-known for his _____ and _____ .
4. _____ between hostile nations is unlikely when the _____ is reduced to a mere murmur by an attitude of _____ and a complacent acceptance of the _____ .

B.

cuaze celery	baah raleif
exo poste fact	mole-dum-err
couniosuer	cammeoflege
buono fidey	numb do plumb
encoggnitto	coorp delicati
horsey-d'ovure	fassad

1. To hide from his enemies, the author wrote under a _____ and, whenever he was in public, went _____ by wearing a _____ .
2. The famous _____ of pop art claimed that the _____ carving on the _____ of the courthouse was a _____ example of Americana.
3. The murder at sea of Amanda Mandala became a _____ because when investigators studied the _____ , they thought at first she had died of an extreme case of _____ but later discovered she had eaten a poisoned _____ .

C.

carpe blanch	peas du resistance
burgoeisee	ala mande
ah priority	errozats
ghourmete	fax pausse
cruissine	add enfenetom
none secreture	goremaund

1. He was a perfect member of the _____ —forever drawing ridiculous _____ but never guilty of a _____ .
2. In a restaurant one can distinguish between a _____ and a _____ by noting which one finishes the meal first.
3. At the Animal Rights League banquet the _____ was an example of vegetarian _____ that was prepared with _____ meat.
4. His _____ assumption was that the dictator, given _____ , would oppress his people _____ .

D.

corps deiumm	all mattar
Zitguest	cool-du-sack
deubut	ecstemprory
graituss	per rota
courtage	pretergge
pre diumb	deubutent
tat-e-tat	vorbertin

1. In a private _____ the old woman and her young _____ discussed the girl's upcoming _____ in high society.
2. The consultant is paid _____ and the amount is divided among all the departments on a _____ basis.
3. During his visit to his _____ , he joined a _____ that marched into the assembly hall.
4. Although it is _____ to sell you the machine gun, I will give it to you _____ .

5. The _____ was asked to give an _____ speech on the _____ of the current era, which she claimed to be " _____ ."

E.

auf rivior	deaf acto
toor du foarse	Wiltenshaunng
en tutu	belley-ladders
in abbscentia	bleitzkrig
ano doimani	batton
viz-a-viz	verrbuttem

1. Reeling from the _____ of Rhett's charming attentions, she surrendered herself _____ and left her former boyfriend without so much as an _____ .
2. With André holding the _____ , the orchestra achieved a stunning _____ performance of the Forgotten Sonatas.
3. We must meet _____ so I can report her statements to you _____ .
4. Robert says he can handle the case _____ , but _____ his record so far proves that he cannot.
5. The _____ s of great men and women are shaped by the depth of their acquaintance with _____ .

F.

creshe	alla cortez
finnis	extra oficia
guauche	alf viederjzhen
litemotive	

1. In Rollo's first short story about Christmas, an old and battered _____ became associated with the _____ of humble reverence.
2. Although distastefully _____ , the country sheriff received an abundance of _____ respect.
3. Reaching the _____ , we say, " _____ ."

CHAPTER TWENTY-ONE

Spelling Abbreviations

The abbreviations below are commonly used in our everyday business, social, and personal lives. Familiarize yourself with useful abbreviations that you may not be presently using.

Days of the Week

Weekday	Abbreviation
Sunday	Sun.
Monday	Mon.
Tuesday	Tues.
Wednesday	Wed.
Thursday	Thur.
Friday	Fri.
Saturday	Sat.

Months of the Year

Month	Abbreviation
January	Jan.
February	Feb.
March	Mar.
April	Apr.
May	May
June	Jun.
July	Jul.
August	Aug.
September	Sep.
October	Oct.
November	Nov.
December	Dec.

Designating Time

By the Calendar	Abbreviation
anno Domini (Latin for "in the year of the Lord")	A.D.
before Christ	B.C.

By the Clock

ante meridiem (Latin for "before noon")	A.M.
post meridiem (Latin for "after noon")	P.M.
Greenwich Mean Time	G.M.T.
Central Standard Time	C.S.T.
Eastern Standard Time	E.S.T.
Mountain Standard Time	M.S.T.
Pacific Standard Time	P.S.T.

Standard Measurements

Term	Abbreviation
bushel	bu.
dozen	doz.
foot	ft.
hour	hr.
inch	in.
ounce	oz.
pound	lb.
yard	yd.
year	yr.

Metric Measurements

Term	Abbreviation
centimeter	cm.
kilogram	kg.
kilometer	km.
liter	l.
milligram	mg.
millimeter	mm.

Personal Titles

Title	Abbreviation
Assistant	Asst.
Doctor	Dr.
Doctor of Dental Surgery	D.D.S.
Doctor of Medicine	M.D.
Doctor of Philosophy	Ph.D.
Esquire	Esq.
Governor	Gov.
Honorable	Hon.
Junior	Jr.
Lieutenant	Lt.
President	Pres.
Professor	Prof.
Registered Nurse	R.N.
Reverend	Rev.
Senior	Sr.

Business Names

Term	Abbreviation
Association	Assn.
Brothers	Bros.
Department	Dept.
Incorporated	Inc.
Limited	Ltd.
Manufacturing	Mfg.

Postal Terms

Term	Abbreviation
Avenue	Ave.
Building	Bldg.
Boulevard	Blvd.
Collect on Delivery	C.O.D.
Free on Board	F.O.B.
Number	No.

Post Office	P.O.
received	recd.
Rural Free Delivery	R.F.D.
Street	St.

State Abbreviations

State	Abbreviation
Alabama	AL
Alaska	AK
Arizona	AZ
Arkansas	AR
California	CA
Colorado	CO
Connecticut	CT
Delaware	DE
District of Columbia	DC
Florida	FL
Georgia	GA
Hawaii	HI
Idaho	ID
Illinois	IL
Indiana	IN
Iowa	IA
Kansas	KS
Kentucky	KY
Louisiana	LA
Maine	ME
Maryland	MD

State	Abbreviation
Massachusetts	MA
Michigan	MI
Minnesota	MN
Mississippi	MS
Missouri	MO
Montana	MT
Nebraska	NE
Nevada	NV
New Hampshire	NH
New Jersey	NJ
New Mexico	NM
New York	NY
North Carolina	NC
North Dakota	ND
Ohio	OH
Oklahoma	OK
Oregon	OR
Pennsylvania	PA
Puerto Rico	PR
Rhode Island	RI
South Carolina	SC
South Dakota	SD
Tennessee	TN
Texas	TX
Utah	UT
Vermont	VT
Virginia	VA
Washington	WA
West Virginia	WV
Wisconsin	WI
Wyoming	WY

CHAPTER TWENTY-TWO

Solving Your Spelling Problem Forever

The key to solving your spelling problem forever is to stop thinking of it as a *spelling problem*. Instead, think of it as a *vocabulary project*. If you approach the English language as a gold mine of ideas and expressions—rather than a mine field of errors to be nervously avoided—you will find that spelling itself becomes just part of an ongoing process of learning to communicate more clearly and expressively.

Estimates of the average person's "working" vocabulary range from 4,000 to 12,000 words. However, we don't have *one* vocabulary, we have *four*: a speaking vocabulary, a writing vocabulary, a reading vocabulary, and a recognition vocabulary. These vocabularies are like concentric circles of word comprehension, with the speaking vocabulary the smallest circle and the recognition vocabulary the largest. People who read extensively may have recognition vocabularies exceeding 50,000 words.

○ Our **speaking vocabulary** is the most limited of our vocabularies. It consists only of words we use in conversation.

○ Our **writing vocabulary** is more extensive than our speaking vocabulary. If

PART SIX

BECOMING A BETTER WORDSMITH

we have a wide reading background, it can consist of many thousands more words than the speaking vocabulary.

○ Our **reading vocabulary** includes both our speaking and our writing vocabularies, plus more. It contains words that we can define when we see them, even though we don't usually use them in conversation or writing.

○ Our **recognition vocabulary** contains words that we have seen or heard previously but cannot clearly define. We probably recognize them in context, but we aren't confident that we know their precise meaning.

Thus, the process of *vocabulary building* consists of transferring words from our reading and recognition vocabularies into our speaking and writing vocabularies. Many roads lead to a strong vocabulary, and the remaining chapters in this section map several of them.

Here is a general summary of methods you should use to build your vocabulary—and your mastery of spelling:

○ Learn only words that you intend to use.
○ Keep a notebook or file card collection of new words.
○ Use the dictionary.
○ Try to recognize the use of the word in context.
○ Learn roots, prefixes, and suffixes.
○ Build word families by converting each new word into other parts of speech.
○ Investigate word origins and changes in word meaning.
○ Study your words daily and use them in writing and speaking.

Becoming a Good Speller

This book has been carefully planned to help you become a good speller. But you must do your part. Here are some ways you can help yourself:

1. *Don't think of yourself as a poor speller.* Many people—to escape embarrassment—even boast of their inability to spell. This can be harmful. Face the reality of your problem and begin to solve it by forming good habits. You must work in order to learn.
2. *Keep a notebook for vocabulary building and spelling improvement.* In it, record each word that you misspell; copy it neatly, carefully, using the dictionary to doublecheck for accuracy. Put only one word per page. Use the rest of the page to enter the following information from your dictionary:

○ Spelling, syllabification, and pronunciation
○ Part of speech; use as other part(s) of speech
○ Origin (etymology), roots
○ Meanings
○ Synonyms, antonyms

Then copy out the sentence in which you found the word. Be sure to leave space for other sentences you may come upon or examples of how you have heard the word used in speaking.

Finally, study the new word frequently. Make a point of finding occasions where you can use the word in speaking and writing. Drill on new words over and over until they are absolutely learned. A score of 98 percent in spelling is not enough—you can do better. Your goal must be perfection.

3. *Analyze your difficulty.* Does it stem from
   - carelessness in writing, reading, listening, or pronunciation?
   - confusion about similar words that are spelled differently?
   - misunderstanding word meanings in context?
   - mistakes with suffixes, hyphens, or apostrophes?

Eliminate the difficulty by studying the particular chapter in this book that deals with your particular problem.

4. *Don't try to study too many words at one time.* It is better to concentrate your attention on memorizing small batches of words. Be 100 percent confident that you *absolutely* know how to correctly spell all the words in a small batch before you move on to the next.

Just stick to your vocabulary-building discipline and you will be amazed at how much your spelling improves!

CHAPTER TWENTY-THREE

Using Your Ear

In English, there is no such thing as a "correct" pronunciation in the sense that the answer to an arithmetic problem is correct. There is no *one* right way to say a word. Instead, we should think of pronunciation as being "acceptable" or "unacceptable"— that is, good usage or not.

A pronunciation is acceptable in the United States if it meets the following requirements:

○ *It is native, not foreign.* Good English is not spoken with a foreign accent. In any area with large numbers of immigrants, you must be careful about unconsciously adopting foreignisms.

○ *It is native American, not British.* For a person born in the United States to affect a Cockney or an Oxford accent is downright silly.

○ *It is characteristic of an entire region of the United States, not some small locality, such as a town.* Coastal New England, the Middle Atlantic area, the coastal and mountainous South, the West—these are examples of regions with their own variations of pronunciation. No one region is superior to others in pronunciation. A New Yorker should not attempt to talk like a Texan, nor a Texan like a resident of Maine.

○ *It is used by educated and cultured people.* We should take as guides those who know something about the language and treat it with respect.

○ *It is modern.* Pronunciations change, and there isn't much sense in adopting a pronunciation that was popular five hundred years ago or one we think will be popular twenty-five years hence.

From these criteria, it is clear that more than one pronunciation of a word may be acceptable—that is, good usage. However, any pronunciation that is foreign, provincial, pedantic, affected, or obsolete must be considered unacceptable—that is, bad usage.

Using Your Ear to Become a Better Speller

The phonetic key used in this book to indicate word pronunciation is presented and explained in the **Introduction**. By this point, you should be familiar with the simple system of phonetic respelling used thus far. The most common spelling problems that come up because of incorrect or slurred pronunciation of words, syllables, and letters are covered in **Chapter 6: Lost-and-Found Sounds**. This chapter focuses on the role of accent on pronunciation—and the relationship between part of speech and accent placement in pronunciation. Often, paying attention to placement of the primary accent in a word can help us "find" lost vowel and consonant sounds—and thereby improve our spelling. And since many words can change grammatical function (part of speech) with little or no change of form, the shift of the primary accent from one syllable to another—along with the word's position in the sentence—are the key to recognizing which function the word is serving.

Certain words are accented on the first syllable when used as nouns or adjectives, on the second when used as verbs. Here are a few examples:

	Noun or Adjective	Verb
absent	AB-sent	ab-SENT
addict	AD-ikt	a-DIKT
annex	AN-eks	a-NEKS
perfect	PUR-fekt	per-FEKT

Other words that shift accent in this way are:

collect	export	project
combat	import	rebel
combine	imprint	record
compound	incense	reject
conduct	increase	subject
contract	permit	survey
convert	prefix	suspect
desert	present	transfer
digest	produce	transport
escort	progress	

In words like those above, the syllables retain basically the same sound, even when the accent shifts. However, in certain words the shift of accent is accompanied by a phonetic change as well. Here are some illustrations:

	Noun or Adjective	Verb
attribute	AT-ri-bewt	a-TRIB-yewt
consummate	kon-SUM-it	KON-su-mayt
perfume	PUR-fyewm (n.)	per-FYEWM
	per-FYEWM (adj.)	
refuse	REF-yews	re-FYEWZ
compact	kom-PAKT (n. *or* adj.)	kom-PAKT
	KOM-pakt (adj.)	

Other words shift accent and sometimes change in other areas of pronunciation when the part of speech shifts from noun to adjective or adjective to adverb. For example:

adept	AD-ept (n.)	a-DEPT (adj.)
cleanly	KLEN-lee (adj.)	KLEEN-lee (adv.)

When certain words ending in **-ate** are used as verbs, this last syllable is pronounced **AYT**. But when they are used as adjectives or nouns, the final vowel is indeterminate in quality and the syllable resembles **IT**. Here are two examples:

	Noun or Adjective	Verb
advocate	AD-vo-kit	AD-vo-kayt
aggregate	AG-re-git	AG-re-gayt

Other words that shift pronunciation in this way are:

alternate	deliberate	intimate
appropriate	designate	moderate
approximate	desolate	predicate
associate	duplicate	separate
degenerate	estimate	
delegate	graduate	

Note, however, that prostrate is pronounced PROS-trayt both as a verb and as an adjective.

The four-syllable adjectives ending in **-able** are frequently mispronounced—and thus frequently misspelled. The mistaken tendency is to accent them on the second syllable, usually following the accent pattern of the word from which the adjective was formed. For example: **admirable** should be pronounced AD-mir-a-b'l *not* ad-MY-ra-b'l. All the following adjectives are correctly accented on the first syllable:

	Say	Not
amicable	AM-i-ka-b'l	a-MIK-a-b'l
applicable	AP-li-ka-b'l	a-PLIK-a-b'l
comparable	KOM-pa-ra-b'l	kom-PAYR-a-b'l
equitable	EK-wit-a-b'l	e-KWIT-a-b'l
formidable	FAWR-mid-a-b'l	fawr-MID-a-b'l
lamentable	LAM-en-ta-b'l	la-MENT-a-b'l
preferable	PREF-ur-a-b'l	pre-FUR-a-b'l
reputable	REP-yew-ta-b'l	re-PYEW-ta-b'l

When the word is preceded by a prefix like **-ir**, the accent remains on the root, although it is now the second syllable of the word. Some examples:

	Say	Not
irreparable	i-REP-a-ra-b'l	i-re-PAYR-a-b'l
irrevocable	i-REV-o-ka-b'l	i-re-VOH-ka-b'l

Use this information about how sound and function correspond with each other in many English words to put your ear to work for you as a speller.

CHAPTER TWENTY-FOUR

Using the Dictionary

"I have a dictionary, but how can I find a word there when I don't know how to spell it?"

You have probably asked this question more times than you care to remember. Obviously, it would be easier to find a troublesome word if you knew how to spell it— but then you wouldn't need the dictionary to look it up! Actually, it isn't as difficult as you might think to locate a word that you aren't sure how to spell. A few Sherlock Holmes-style deductions, a few simple next-best-thing strategies, and you will find the word you are searching for. And if you are a serious student of the language, that will probably be the last time you have to look *that* word up. By using the wordsmith techniques discussed in this section of the book, you will master all the words that once were problematic.

How do you use your dictionary to learn spelling? Let's use an example: Tomorrow you plan to attend a particular kind of party—a "supprise" party. "Supprise" is your first guess, but knowing it to be merely a guess, you consult your dictionary. Of course, you can't find such a word. Now what? Maybe dropping a **p**—"suprise." No, that leaves you right where you were— nowhere, and without a clue about which direction to go.

Now try this technique, step-by-step:

○ **First, pronounce the word aloud— syllable by syllable.** Ah, *now* you hear the **r** sound that gets lost when we don't give careful attention to pronunciation.

○ **Second, make several more guesses and write them down.** You probably come up with "surprise" and "surprize." Since the first syllable in both alternatives is **sur-**, you know the general vicinity you should be heading toward. Your only problem now is the second syllable—**-prise** or **-prize**. Your dictionary will solve that problem quickly: **surprise**.

○ **Third, if none of your guesses is correct, look for another word that is related in meaning.** In the case of **surprise**, this step isn't very useful—since all the similar words are *more complicated* than **surprise**. If you had been searching for **amaze** or **astound**, you might have tried looking for **surprise** (they are listed as synonyms following the definition). Here's a different example: If you were having trouble finding the word **fowl**, you could look for **chicken**, which is defined as "a domestic *fowl*."

○ **Fourth, copy the correct spelling in your vocabulary notebook or on an index card,** following the guidelines covered in **Chapter 23: Solving Your Spelling Problem Forever.** The only way to develop mastery over the spelling of **surprise**—or **fowl**—is to *not* let it slip out of your attention. Put in the concentrated effort required to take the "trouble" out of your troublesome words.

How to Get the Most from Your Dictionary

To progress more rapidly toward spelling mastery, you must include a good abridged dictionary in your reference library. Also, you must learn how to use your dictionary effectively. Study the sample pages from the *Doubleday Dictionary* on pages 165-166. You will notice that dictionaries provide much more than information on spelling. Indeed, almost every chapter in this book has used material from dictionaries. Your dictionary will help you learn:

○ accurate pronunciation of words
○ correct syllabification of words
○ correct use of capitals, hyphens, italics, etc.
○ the history and etymology of words
○ the meaning or meanings of words
○ synonyms and antonyms
○ correct word usage

Follow this treasure map to the riches of information to be found on the pages of your dictionary:

GUIDE WORDS are shown in large type at the top of each page and indicate the first and last entries on that page.

SYLLABIFICATION is indicated by syllabic dots dividing main entry words.

MAIN ENTRY is shown in boldface type and consists of words, phrases, or abbreviations, prefixes, suffixes, and combining forms.

PRONUNCIATION is shown in parentheses and follows the main entry in phonetic equivalent.

INFLECTED FORMS are given when there is an irregularity of form—for the present participle of verbs, the plural of nouns, and the comparative and superlative of adjectives and adverbs.

USAGE information is included in italics preceding the particular part of the definition to which it applies.

HOMOGRAPHS are words identical in spelling but with different meanings and origins and, sometimes, pronunciation. They are differentiated by a superscript numeral, as in $slop^1$ and $slop^2$.

DEFINITION is the meaning. The order in which the different senses of the word are listed is based on the frequency of their usage.

ILLUSTRATION is sometimes included to clarify the definitions.

RUN-ON ENTRY is a word derived from other words by addition or replacement of a suffix—syllabified and stressed where needed.

ETYMOLOGY is indicated in brackets following the definition, giving the origin of the word when it came into the English language.

PART OF SPEECH follows the pronunciation; the labels in italics are abbreviated as follows: n. (noun), vt. (verb-transitive), vi. (verb-intransitive), adj. (adjective), adv. (adverb), prep. (preposition), conj. (conjunction), and interj. (interjection).

GUIDE WORDS —

are shown in large type at the top of each page and indicate the first and last entries on that page.

(**slippery**)

slip·per·y (slip′ər-ē) *adj.* **·per·i·er, ·per·i·est 1** Having a surface so smooth that bodies slip or slide easily on it. **2** That evades one's grasp; elusive. **3** Unreliable; tricky. —**slip′per·i·ness** *n.*

slippery elm 1 A species of small elm with mucilaginous inner bark. **2** Its wood or inner bark.

slip·shod (slip′shod′) *adj.* **1** Wearing shoes or slippers down at the heels. **2** Slovenly; sloppy. **3** Performed carelessly: *slipshod* work.

SYLLABICATION —

is indicated by syllabic dots dividing main entry words.

(**slip·stream**) (slip′strēm′) *n. Aeron.* The stream of air driven backwards by the propeller of an aircraft.

slip-up (slip′up′) *n. Informal* A mistake; error.

slit (slit) *n.* A relatively straight cut or a long, narrow opening. —*v.t.* **slit, slit·ting 1** To make a long incision in; slash. **2** To cut lengthwise into strips. **3** To sever. [ME *slitten*] —**slit′ter** *n.*

slith·er (slith′ər) *v.i.* **1** To slide; slip, as on a loose surface. **2** To glide, as a snake. —*v.t.* **3** To cause to slither. —*n.* A sinuous, gliding movement. [<OE *slidrian*] —**slith′er·y** *adj.*

MAIN ENTRY —

is shown in boldface type and consists of words, phrases or abbreviations, prefixes, suffixes and combining forms.

(**sliv·er**) (sliv′ər) *n.* **1** A slender piece, as of wood, cut or torn off lengthwise; a splinter. **2** Corded textile fibers drawn into a fleecy strand. —*v.t. & v.i.* To cut or be split into long thin pieces. [<ME *sliven* to cleave] —**sliv′er·er** *n.*

slob (slob) *n.* **1** Mud; mire. **2** *Slang* A careless or unclean person. [<Ir. *slab*]

PRONUNCIATION —

is shown in parenthesis and follows the main entry in phonetic equivalent.

(**slob·ber**) (slob′ər) *v.t.* **1** To wet with liquids oozing from the mouth. **2** To shed or spill, as liquid food, in eating. —*v.i.* **3** To drivel; slaver. **4** To talk or act gushingly. —*n.* **1** Liquid spilled as from the mouth. **2** Gushing, sentimental talk. [ME *sloberen*] —**slob′ber·er** *n.* —**slob′ber·y** *adj.*

sloe (slō) *n.* **1** A small, plumlike, astringent fruit. **2** The shrub that bears it; the blackthorn. [<OE *slā*]

sloe gin A cordial with a gin base, flavored with sloes.

INFLECTED FORMS —

are given when there is an irregularity of form, and present participle of verbs, the plural of nouns, and the comparative and superlative of adjectives and adverbs.

slog (slog) *v.t. & v.i.* (**slogged, slog·ging**) **1** To slug, as a pugilist. **2** To plod (one's way). —*n.* A heavy blow. [?] —**slog′ger** *n.*

slo·gan (slō′gən) *n.* **1** A catchword or motto adopted by a political party, advertiser, etc. **2** A battle or rallying cry. [<Scot. Gael. *sluagh* army + *gairm* yell]

USAGE —

information is included when an integral part of definition follows a colon after the particular meaning to which it applies.

slo·gan·eer (slō′gə-nir′) (*Informal*) *n.* One who coins or uses slogans. —*v.i.* To coin or use slogans.

sloop (sloōp) *n.* A small sailboat with a single mast and at least one jib. [<Du. *sloep*]

HOMOGRAPH —

is a word identical in spelling, having different meanings and origins and, sometimes, pronunciation. It is differentiated by a superior figure such as slop¹ and slop².

(**slop¹**) (slop) *v.* **slopped, slop·ping** *v.t.* **1** To splash or spill. **2** To walk or move through slush. —*v.t.* **3** To cause (a liquid) to spill or splash. **4** To feed (a domestic animal) with slops. —**slop over 1** To overflow and splash. **2** *Slang* To show too much zeal, emotion, etc. —*n.* **1** Slush or watery mud. **2** An unappetizing liquid or watery food. **3** *pl.* Refuse liquid. **4** *pl.* Waste food or swill. [<ME *sloppe* mud]

(**slop²**) (slop) **1** A loose outer garment, as a smock. **2** *pl.* Articles of clothing and other merchandise sold to sailors on shipboard. [ME *sloppe*]

Sloop

slug

an organization, or a place in a sequence. —*v.t.* **slot·ted,
slot·ting** To cut a slot or slots in. [<OF *esclot* the hollow
between the breasts]

sloth (slôth, slōth, sloth) *n.* **1** Disinclination to exertion;
laziness. **2** Any of several slow-
moving, arboreal mammals of
South America. [<SLOW]

— DEFINITION
is the meaning. The order in which the
different senses of the word are listed is
based on frequency of usage.

sloth·ful (slôth′fəl, slōth′-,
sloth′-) *adj.* Inclined to or characterized by sloth. —**sloth′ful·ly** *adv.*
—**sloth′ful·ness** *n.* —Syn. lazy, in-
dolent, sluggish, shiftless.

slot machine A vending machine or gambling machine having a slot in which a coin is
dropped to cause operation.

Three-toed sloth

ILLUSTRATION
to clarify the definitions.

slouch (slouch) *v.i.* **1** To have a
downcast or drooping gait, look, or posture. **2** To hang or
droop carelessly. —*n.* **1** A drooping movement or appearance caused by depression or carelessness. **2** An awkward
or incompetent person. [?] —**slouch′y** *adj.* (**·i·er, ·i·est**) —
slouch′i·ly *adv.* —**slouch′i·ness** *n.*

— RUN-ON ENTRY
is a word derived from other words by
addition or replacement of a suffix, syllabified and stressed where needed.

slough¹ (slou; slōō *esp. for def.* 2) *n.* **1** A place of deep mud
or mire. **2** A stagnant swamp, backwater, etc. **3** A state of
great despair or degradation. [<OE *slōh*] —**slough′y** *adj.*
slough² (sluf) *n.* **1** Dead tissue separated and thrown off
from living tissue. **2** The skin of a serpent that has been
or is about to be shed. —*v.t.* **1** To cast off; shed. **2** To dis-
card; shed, as a habit or a growth. —*v.i.* **3** To be cast off.
4 To cast off a slough or tissue. [ME *slouh*] —**slough′y** *adj.*

— ETYMOLOGY
is indicated in brackets following the definition giving the origin of the word when
it came into the English language.

Slo·vak (slō′väk, slō′vak) *n.* **1** One of a Slavic people of
NW Hungary and parts of Moravia. **2** The language spoken by the Slovaks. —*adj.* Of or pertaining to the Slovaks
or to their language. Also **Slo·vak′i·an.**
slov·en (sluv′ən) *n.* One who is habitually untidy, careless, or dirty. [ME *sloveyn*]
Slo·vene (slō′vēn, slō·vēn′) *n.* One of a group of S Slavs
now living in NW Yugoslavia. —*adj.* Of or pertaining to
the Slovenes or to their language. —**Slo·ve′ni·an** *(adj., n.)*

— PART OF SPEECH
follow the pronunciation, and the labels
in italics are abbreviated as follows: n.
(noun), v. (verb-transitive), v.i. (verb-
intransitive), adj. (adjective), adv. (adverb), prep. (preposition), conj. (conjunction), and interj. (interjection).

slov·en·ly (sluv′ən·lē) *adj.* **·i·er, ·i·est** Untidy and careless in appearance, work, habits, etc. —*adv.* In a slovenly
manner. —**slov′en·li·ness** *n.*
slow (slō) *adj.* **1** Taking a long time to move, perform, or
occur. **2** Behind the standard time: said of a timepiece. **3**
Not hasty: *slow* to anger. **4** Dull in comprehension: a *slow*
student. **5** Uninteresting; tedious: a *slow* drama. **6** Denoting a condition of a racetrack that retards the horses′
speed. **7** Heating or burning slowly; low: a *slow* flame. **8**
Not brisk; slack: Business is *slow.* —*v.t. & v.i.* To make or
become slow or slower: often with *up* or *down.* —*adv.* In
a slow manner. [<OE *slāw*] —**slow′ly** *adv.* —**slow′ness** *n.*
slow-mo·tion (slō′mō′shən) *adj.* **1** Moving or acting at
less than normal speed. **2** Denoting a television or motion
picture filmed at greater than standard speed so that the
action appears slow in normal projection.
sludge (sluj) *n.* **1** Soft, water-soaked mud. **2** A slush of
snow or broken or half-formed ice. **3** Muddy or pasty
refuse, sediment, etc. [?] —**sludg′y** *adj.* (**·i·er, ·i·est**)
slue¹ (slōō) *v.* **slued, slu·ing** *v.t.* **1** To cause to swing, slide,
or skid to the side. **2** To cause to twist or turn. —*v.i.* **3** To

Dictionary excerpts from THE DOUBLEDAY
DICTIONARY. Copyright © 1975, Doubleday
& Co., Inc., Garden City, New York. Reprinted
by the permission of the publisher.

CHAPTER TWENTY-FIVE

Using Memory Devices

Throughout this book you have learned that the word to be spelled is more important than any rule. Nevertheless, by applying some basic principles of spelling, pronunciation, and word formation, you have already mastered the spelling of a considerable number of troublesome words. In this final chapter you can learn how to add certain memorization techniques to your arsenal of weapons for combating poor spelling.

Memory devices (known as mnemonics, from Greek, meaning "to remember") are techniques of memory association. With a mnemonic device you create a special connection between the word (or parts of the word) and one or more ideas or sensations. For instance, you might help yourself remember that dessert (meaning "the sweet course at the end of a meal") has **two s**'s by thinking that you wouldn't mind having **two desserts**. Other, similar techniques are described below.

Mnemonic devices work in a highly personal way. Our neural pathways—and our particular memories, thinking styles, likes and dislikes—are linked together in patterns unique to us. As a result, what works for one person won't necessarily work for another. We each have to develop our own repertoire of tools and techniques. Basically, there are only two rules governing the use of mnemonic devices:

○ If it works, use it.
○ Keep it simple.

Remember, these memory devices are supposed to *facilitate* your spelling, not substitute for it. When memorizing the mnemonic device takes more time and concentration than simply memorizing the word, you're working the system backward!

With these points in mind, consider the following techniques for remembering how to spell troublesome words:

1. Whenever possible, treat the troublesome word like a puzzle. Reduce it to smaller, simpler words that somehow relate to the thing the word names. This is the same technique as the "two desserts" device. Look at these examples:

- **candidate**—is the candidate **candid**?
- **together**—I want **to get her**
- **modern**—in the modern **mode**
- **business**—it is easy to **sin** in business
- **balloon**—a balloon forms a **ball**
- **costume**—what is the **cost** of the costume?

2. Break the word into syllables and pronounce each syllable—even if the word is not normally pronounced that way. Here are a few examples:

- **fore + head**
- **lab + o + ra + to + ry**
- **hand + ker + chief**
- **hand + some**
- **ex + tra + or + di + nary**
- **or + ches + tra**

3. Associate the word with its origin. Look at these examples:

- **kindergarten**—from German **kinder** ("children") and **garten** ("garden"); a garden of children
- **cafeteria**—from French **café** ("coffee"); a place for coffee
- **exorbitant**—from Latin **ex** ("out of") and **orb** ("world"); in other words, exorbitant prices are "out of this world"
- **grammar**—from Greek **gramma** ("letter"); relating to letters
- **disaster**—from Greek **dis** ("away from") and **aster** ("star"); a falling out of alignment with the stars

4. Create some tricks of your own—visual images, rhymes, snippets of songs or jingles, even puns—that key into the point of confusion regarding the spelling of a particular word. Anything goes:

- **principle**—a princip**LE** is a ru**LE**
- **michievous**—*which*-of-us is not *misch*-of-us?
- **censor**—one who's *sore* about *sin*
- **debt**—I must **b** ("be") in debt
- **cemetery**—we get there with **e**'s ("ease")
- **develop**—*lop* off the final **e**

Develop your own memory devices to get the upper hand with words that always seem to give you trouble.

Core Word Post-Test

The **Final Review Test** in Part I below contains the same fifty words from the core list that were used at the outset of this book in the **Pre-Test**. If you find that your score is perfect—as it should be—do not assume that your task is over, although you are now securely on your way. Spelling needs continuous attention. Continue to review. Construct your own tests. Use your newly mastered words in context. From time to time, test yourself on the **Mastery Tests** in this book. Your attitude toward spelling has much to do with your continued improvement. Accept the challenge and responsibility that are yours. The rewards are immense—and it can be great fun.

Part I: Underline the one correctly spelled word in each of the following groups.

1. loseing, losing, lossing
2. proceed, procede, proseed, prosede
3. hieght, heighth, height, hieghth
4. oppinion, opinion, opinnion, oppinnion
5. writing, writeing, writting, writteing
6. proffessor, profesor, proffesor, professor
7. therefor, therefore, therfor, therfore
8. foriegn, forein, forien, foreign
9. marraige, marridge, marriage, marrage
10. all right, alright, allright, all rite

11. heros, heroez, heroes, herroes
12. refered, referred, reffered, refferred
13. amachoor, amatoor, amatuer, amateur
14. atheist, athiest, atheast, athaest
15. ninty, ninety, ninedy, ninnety
16. advertisement, advertizment, advertisment, advertizement
17. leasure, leesure, leisure, liesure
18. làbratory, laborattory, laboratory, labaratory
19. irestistible, irresistable, irresistible, iresistible
20. discription, description, descripttion, discripttion
21. efficeint, eficient, eficeint, efficient
22. rhythm, rythm, ryrhm, rhytm
23. embarass, embarrass, emberress, emmbarass
24. enviroment, environent, environment, envirronment
25. exaggerate, exagerate, exagerrate, exegarrate
26. prevalent, privelant, preveland, prevelent
27. irrevelant, irrelevant, irrelevent, irelevant
28. ocurence, occurance, occurence, occurrence
29. accidently, accidentaly, accidentally, accidentilly
30. adolesence, adolecense, adolesense, adolescence
31. wierd, weard, weird, weiard
32. advantagous, advantageous, advanttagous, addvantageous
33. paralel, parralel, parallel, paralell
34. imediately, imeddiately, immediately, immediatly
35. beneficcial, benefficial, beneficail, beneficial
36. criticism, criticizm, critticism, critticizm

37. occassion, occasion, ocassion, ocasion
38. lonliness, lonelyness, loneliness, lonlyness
39. charcteristic, chrackteristic, characteristic, characteristick
40. beleif, beleaf, belief, bellief
41. acomodate, accomadate, acommodate, accommodate
42. dissapoint, disappoint, dissappoint, disapoint
43. grammer, gramar, grammar, gramer
44. athelete, atlete, athleet, athlete
45. intrest, interest, interrest, intirest
46. controversial, contraversial, controversail, contriversial
47. separite, seperate, separate, sepparate
48. maintainance, maintenance, maintenence, maintainence
49. arguement, argumment, argument, arrgument
50. villein, villain, villian, villin

Part II: Underline the one correctly spelled word in each of the following groups.

1. amirable, admirible, admirable, admirrable
2. alyin, alien, alein, allien
3. auxiliary, auxlary, auxilliery, auxiliery
4. averse, averce, avoice, averrse
5. beir, bier, biere, beire
6. breef, breif, breaf, brief
7. Birtton, Brittan, Briton, briton
8. casheer, casheir, cashier, cashear
9. cieling, ceiling, cealing, sieling
10. civilian, civilien, civillian, civillain
11. climacktic, climactic, climactik, climectic
12. countarfiet, counterfiet, counterfeit, counterfiat

13. couragous, courageous, courageious, couragus
14. crotchet, crotchit, crotchat, crochit
15. decietful, deceitfull, deceitful, deceatful
16. deign, deagn, daegn, diegn
17. deprecate, depresate, depprecate, depracate
18. desireable, desirrable, desirable, dessirable
19. duely, duly, dooly, dooley
20. eether, eather, either, eyether
21. ilicit, elicit, ellicit, elisit
22. excede, exseed, exceed, exsede
23. exsess, exscess, excess, ekcess
24. facetshous, facetious, fascetious, facetus
25. fiegn, faign, feign, fein
26. feind, fiend, feand, feend
27. fierce, fearce, feirce, feerce
28. fiary, feiry, fiery, fyery
29. gayety, gaiety, gaeity, gayty
30. glashier, glacier, glaceir, glacer
31. greef, grief, greif, greaf
32. likable, likible, likeible, likeable
33. medeval, medeival, medieval, mediaval
34. meen, mein, mien, mian
35. misscheif, mischeif, mischief, mischeef
36. movaible, movable, moveible, movvable
37. naybor, neighbor, niegbor, neigbor
38. neether, neyether, neather, neither
39. outragous, outragious, outrageous, outrageus
40. patient, patiant, pattient, pashient
41. peaceable, peacable, paseable, peaceible
42. picnicing, picniking, picnicking, picniccing
43. peir, pier, peeir, pire
44. profficient, proficient, profishient, proficeint
45. reppreive, repreave, reprieve, repreive
46. siezure, seizure, seasure, seazure
47. slaigh, sliegh, sleigh, slegh
48. straight, streight, striaght, straigt
49. trolleis, trolleys, trollies, troleys
50. paniced, paniked, panicked, panicced

Answers to Exercises

Exercise 1.1

1. mischief
2. deity
3. species
4. deficiency
5. quotient
6. glacier
7. conscience
8. transient
9. foreign
10. receipt
11. financier
12. sobriety
13. shriek
14. veiled
15. seize
16. neighbor
17. reins
18. counterfeit
19. leisure
20. deceitful

Exercise 1.2

1. civilian
2. villain
3. mountain
4. guardian
5. martial
6. auxiliary
7. Christian
8. beneficial
9. chieftain
10. certain
11. Britain
12. genial
13. peculiar
14. partial
15. brilliant

Exercise 1.3

1. exceed
2. procedure
3. preceding
4. success
5. antecedent
6. intercession
7. concede
8. supersede
9. intercede
10. secede

Exercise 2.1

1. dyeing
2. judging
3. toeing
4. argument
5. lovely
6. singeing
7. canoeing
8. advantageous
9. graceful
10. pursuing
11. likelihood
12. desirable
13. changeable
14. truly
15. definitely
16. dying
17. awful
18. serviceable
19. usage
20. dining

Exercise 2.2

1. laid
2. families
3. easily
4. valleys
5. reliance
6. goofiest
7. cries
8. played
9. mysterious
10. marriage
11. hurried
12. merciful
13. daily
14. business
15. annoyed
16. buries
17. journeys
18. dryness
19. relies
20. beauties

Exercise 3.1

1. barring
2. croaked
3. looking
4. mower
5. scrubbed
6. mixing
7. crammed
8. hurting
9. potted
10. moaning

Exercise 3.2

1. inferring
2. amending
3. concealment
4. equipage
5. quarreled
6. repellent
7. existence
8. transmitter
9. considering
10. legalize

Exercise 4.1

1. punches
2. houses
3. ribbons
4. paradoxes
5. giggles
6. albatrosses
7. consumers
8. gazettes
9. infants
10. parishes

Exercise 4.2

1. studios
2. embargoes
3. hooves
4. altos
5. cameos
6. tomatoes
7. briefs
8. wives
9. volcanoes
10. torsos

Exercise 4.3

1. teeth
2. parentheses
3. children
4. headquarters
5. media
6. bases
7. lice
8. foci
9. synopses
10. addenda

Exercise 4.4

1. commanders in chief
2. Justins
3. handfuls
4. P's
5. Washingtons
6. lieutenant colonels
7. 5's
8. M.D.'s
9. courts-martial
10. classrooms

Exercise 4.5

1. slept — slept
2. laughed — laughed
3. grew — grown
4. delayed — delayed
5. cost — cost
6. reminded — reminded
7. worried — worried
8. hid — hidden
9. slapped — slapped
10. thought — thought
11. dignified — dignified
12. rose — risen
13. cut — cut
14. bribed — bribed
15. drew — drawn

Exercise 6.1

1. violets
2. jewels
3. acquaintances
4. all right
5. incidentally
6. strength
7. privilege
8. district
9. background
10. separate

Exercise 6.2

1. partner
2. irrelevant
3. escape
4. beside
5. pattern
6. cavalry
7. washing
8. exactly
9. diary
10. mischievous

Exercise 7.1

1. wrestle
2. reign
3. failure
4. knock
5. blame
6. calculate
7. honorable
8. fudge
9. solemn
10. listen

Exercise 7.2

1. attraction
2. belligerent
3. hemisphere
4. appearance
5. cinnamon
6. collage
7. bottle
8. different
9. suggestion
10. succumb

Exercise 8.1

1. excess
2. accept
3. adjoins
4. adverse
5. advise
6. affected
7. aisle
8. aloud
9. ally
10. already, all together

Exercise 8.2

1. illusion
2. alter
3. angel
4. assent
5. assistance
6. birth
7. besides
8. bloc
9. bored
10. border

Exercise 8.3

1. break
2. breathe
3. bridle
4. Briton
5. Calvary
6. canvassed
7. capitol
8. censured
9. cord
10. site

Exercise 8.4

1. climatic
2. cloths
3. coarse
4. complement
5. correspondence
6. corps
7. counsel
8. crotchets
9. croquette
10. current

Exercise 8.5

1. dairy
2. deprecates
3. descent
4. desert
5. devise
6. dye
7. dining
8. duel
9. elicit
10. immigrants

Exercise 8.6

1. eminent
2. ensure
3. envelop
4. feinted
5. flair
6. formerly
7. fourth
8. foul
9. gait
10. here

Exercise 8.7

1. herds
2. heirs
3. heroin
4. hoard
5. hostile
6. idle
7. incidence
8. ingenuous
9. instance
10. its

Exercise 8.8

1. latter
2. led
3. lessen
4. liable
5. lightening
6. lone
7. lose
8. maybe
9. minor
10. missal

Exercise 8.9

1. morale
2. muscle
3. naval
4. past
5. patience
6. peace
7. peddle
8. personnel
9. peel
10. presence

Exercise 8.10

1. principal
2. quite
3. rein
4. raze
5. respectively
6. reviewed
7. right
8. rode
9. role
10. saie

Exercise 8.11

1. serge
2. sheer
3. shone
4. sore
5. stationary
6. stature
7. straits
8. tail
9. taut
10. teems

Exercise 8.12

1. than
2. they're
3. threw
4. too
5. vein
6. vain
7. voracious
8. vile
9. waste

Exercise 8.13

1. wait
2. weak
3. whether
4. were
5. we're
6. which
7. whose
8. you're

Exercise 10.1

1. dissonance
2. misshapen
3. mishap
4. commendation
5. dissuaded
6. disappointed
7. misprint
8. misspoke
9. commissioner
10. dissimilar

Exercise 10.2

1. antecedents
2. persist
3. divulge
4. antiseptic
5. precedes
6. professor
7. antidote
8. disease
9. description
10. despair

Exercise 10.3

1. admix
2. allergic
3. dilate
4. disperse
5. impound
6. initial
7. irritable
8. impassive
9. subversion
10. suffocate

Exercise 11.1

1. cura**ble**
2. intang**ible**
3. invinc**ible**
4. deplor**able**
5. plaus**ible**
6. irasc**ible**
7. demonstr**able**
8. immov**able**
9. inaud**ible**
10. vis**ible**

Exercise 11.2

1. Adolesc**ence**
2. subsist**ence**
3. interfer**ence**
4. persist**ent**
5. ignor**ant**
6. extravag**ance**
7. toler**ant**
8. hesit**ant**
9. refer**ence**
10. insist**ence**, resist**ance**

Exercise 11.3

1. accidentally
2. brutal
3. clerical
4. kernel
5. truthfully
6. proposal
7. sizzle
8. logically
9. fatal
10. parcel

Exercise 11.4

1. chastise
2. debtors
3. beautify
4. criticize
5. consumer
6. collar
7. testify
8. employer
9. liquefy
10. spectator

Exercise 12.1

1. bouy-ant
2. okay
3. eventu-ally
4. okay (chang-ing is acceptable)
5. coun-try
6. okay
7. okay
8. crit-icism
9. okay
10. okay

Exercise 12.2

1. well-preserved
2. okay
3. self-assured
4. jack-in-the-box
5. okay
6. wait-and-see
7. okay
8. anti-China
9. okay
10. co-owner

Answers to Mastery Tests

Mastery Test: Chapter 1

Part I
1. civilian
2. succeed
3. perceive
4. beneficial
5. patient
6. intercede
7. notoriety
8. procedure
9. exceed
10. chieftain
11. sheik
12. villain
13. omniscience
14. proceed
15. inveigh
16. precede
17. sleight
18. antecedent
19. supersede
20. Christian

Part II
1. fierce
2. deficient
3. genial
4. hygiene
5. peculiar
6. succession
7. conceit
8. foreign
9. Britain
10. achieve

Mastery Test: Chapter 2

Part I
1. turkey
2. employ
3. relay
4. chimney
5. convey

Part II
1. shoe
2. guarantee
3. eye
4. singe
5. decree

Part III
1. movable
2. finest
3. carrying
4. clumsily
5. management
6. tasteless
7. defiance
8. studious
9. truly
10. advantageous
11. envious
12. woeful
13. denying
14. paid
15. politeness
16. divinity
17. lovable
18. sassier
19. surely
20. arrangement

Mastery Test: Chapter 3

Part I
1. adapt
2. pretend
3. disown
4. creak
5. stoop
6. tempt
7. offend
8. murmur
9. accustom
10. stiff
6. inhabitable
7. conference
8. garlicky
9. youthfully
10. trimness

Part II
1. plainness
2. planetary
3. goddess
4. acquittal
5. equally

Part III
1. forbidding
2. writing
3. occurrence
4. enveloped
5. mimicked
6. mannish
7. boiling
8. partially
9. counseled
10. regretted

Mastery Test: Chapter 4

Part I
1. flashes
2. Negroes
3. scissors
4. curricula
5. teaspoonfuls
6. mottoes
7. cameos
8. strata
9. crises
10. runners-up
11. quartzes
12. altos
13. roofs
14. wolves
15. masses
16. buffalo
17. matches
18. themselves
19. wives
20. fungi

Part II
1. drunk
2. burst
3. sworn
4. began
5. stung
6. dealt
7. flown
8. laid, lay
9. drowned
10. awoke

Mastery Test: Chapter 5

Part I

1. The city of Nome, Alaska, acquired its name through error. There was a small prospectors' settlement known as Anvil City on the Seward Peninsula in Alaska. A Washington clerk drawing a map did not know its name and wrote "Name?" at that place on the map. One of his superiors took the word for "Nome" and that name still stands.

2. *Myths for the Modern*, edited by Philip Corey and William Rogers, was published by Avon Books. Perhaps the best story in it is "Odysseus of the 80's" by Mark Schultz. In this adaptation of Homeric legend, a modern Odysseus drives a Cadillac and drinks Perrier. Unlike his Greek namesake, this hero is no hero at all—just a yuppie trying to win the rat race.

3. What is Africa to me:
Copper sun or scarlet sea,
Jungle star or jungle track,
Strong bronzed men, or regal black
Women from whose loins I sprang
When the birds of Eden sang?
(from "Heritage" by Countee Cullen)

4. It is the grace of God that urges missionaries to suffer the most disheartening privations for the faith. This grace moved St. Isaac Jogues to say (when he came to Canada), "I felt as if it were a Christmas day for me and that I was to be born again to a new life, to a life in Him."

5. When the South seceded from the United States—and thereby sparked the Civil War—the leaders of the Confederacy could not have known the devastation that the conflict would cause both sides. More American lives were lost in the War Between the States than in both World War I and World War II combined. After General Lee surrendered at Appomattox, the Stars and Stripes flew once again over a union of states, but the division of spirits lasted until the turn of the century.

Mastery Test: Chapter 6

Part I	Part II
1. strictly	1. e
2. governor	2. i
3. surprise	3. e
4. accidentally	4. i
5. interest	5. o
6. miniature	6. o
7. hundred	7. e
8. prevail	8. e
9. cruel	9. i
10. complimentary	10. i
11. February	11. i
12. hindrance	12. e
13. perspire	13. i
14. mathematic	14. e
15. disastrous	15. a

Mastery Test: Chapter 7

Part I	Part II
1. h	1. rabble
2. l	2. succotash
3. st	3. riddance
4. ght	4. guffaw
5. gh	5. sluggish
6. sc	6. infallible
7. kn, dg	7. pummel
8. ps	8. connive
9. d	9. appease
10. mn	10. terrestrial
11. wr	11. tissue
12. bt	12. whittle
13. j	13. drizzle
14. ght	14. eccentric
15. rh	15. mammary

Mastery Test: Chapter 8

1. bridal, role, personal, Whether, it's, presents, clothes, patience, morale, compliments, reigns, altar
2. dining, fowl, peel, piece, croquette's, effect, loose, currants, dessert, border, petals, all ready, flair
3. team, muscles, weak, waists, too, weight, tails, then, fourth, breathe, vain, fainted, adverse, minor, soreness

4. led, hostile, hordes, council, course, accept, incidents, ally, device, missile, straight, corps, lesson
5. principle, stature, respectfully, veraciously, shown, elicited, raised, personal, taught, access, right, illusions, ascent, eminence

Mastery Test: Chapter 9

Part I

1. e
2. c
3. a
4. j
5. g
6. d
7. f
8. i
9. b
10. h

4. trans**port**
5. ag**gress**ion
6. **voc**abulary
7. suf**fer**
8. **spec**imen
9. **aut**onomous
10. pre**dict**
11. **anim**osity
12. res**trict**
13. **fac**ility
14. **capa**city
15. contro**vers**y
16. pro**logue**
17. parti**cip**ate
18. se**cede**
19. im**medi**ate
20. **sed**ation

Part II

1. o**miss**ion
2. **gener**ate
3. hier**archy**

Mastery Test: Chapter 10

1. **bene**volence, **bene**ficiary, **bene**diction
2. **cata**pult, **cata**ract
3. **inter**mediate, **inter**rupt, **inter**cept
4. **pre**monition, **pre**text, **pre**serve
5. **fore**cast, **fore**boding, **fore**ground
6. **con**cur, **con**tract, **con**spire
7. **sur**mount, **sur**render, **sur**face
8. **uni**versal, **uni**que, **uni**son
9. **ex**terior, **ex**tinction, **ex**haust, **ex**cerpt
10. **equi**valent, **equi**nox, **equi**librium

Mastery Test: Chapter 11

Part I

1. human**ize**
2. element**ary**
3. acquaint**ance**
4. indicat**or**
5. digest**ible**
6. professio**nally**
7. swiv**el**
8. calen**dar**
9. indul**gence**
10. commend**able**
11. refu**sal**
12. descend**ant**

13. compro**mise**
14. cemet**ery**
15. cynic**ally**
16. antagon**ize**
17. elig**ible**
18. susp**ense**
19. infirm**ary**
20. radia**tor**

Part II

1. peculiar
2. symbolize
3. riddle
4. impertinent
5. perishable
6. squabble
7. honorary
8. permissible
9. sponsor
10. abstinent

Mastery Test: Chapter 12

Part I

1. okay
2. muf-fin
3. okay
4. pas-sage
5. dwin-dling
6. okay
7. okay
8. okay
9. siz-zling
10. exces-sive

Part II

1. pro-United States, middle-road
2. NONE
3. all-night, knee-deep, two-thirds
4. all-cargo, on-time, eighty-six
5. play-off, first-ranked, runner-up
6. President-elect, father-in-law, re-emerged, right-hand
7. A-bomb, ex-President, far-reaching, one-and-only
8. Gun-toting, right-wing, mid-December
9. hand-me-downs, growing-up, nimble-fingered, brand-new
10. Scotch-Irish, one-quarter, one-eighth

Mastery Test: Chapter 13

Part I

1. you'll see
2. they're here
3. here's to health
4. nobody's home
5. they're not sure, they aren't sure
6. I should've gone

7. who's going
8. we can't stay
9. he doesn't drive
10. who could've known

Part II

1. the princesses' gowns
2. Twain's novels
3. Margie and Jeff's home
4. a month's healing
5. a gentlemen's agreement
6. the river's rise
7. the lieutenant colonel's opinion
8. the dogs' leashes
9. the Bauhaus's legacy
10. the days' end

Mastery Test: Chapter 14

A.

1. tariff
2. merchandise, ledger
3. management, franchise
4. auditor, embezzled
5. collateral
6. negotiable
7. personnel

B.

1. promissory, dunning
2. accountant
3. coupons
4. syndicate
5. entrepreneur
6. mortgage, acknowledgment
7. liquidate

C.

1. bigamy, annul, abandonment, alimony
2. annul
3. accessory
4. defendant, alibi
5. indictment, burglary
6. coercion

D.

1. bankrupt, affidavit
2. writ, counselor-at-law
3. subpoena
4. adjudicate
5. bailiff, arraign, homicide
6. usury

Mastery Test: Chapter 15

A.

1. hypertension, barbiturate
2. streptomycin, penicillin, antihistamine
3. amphibian
4. zoology, embryo, botany, fungus

B.

1. carnivorous
2. mammal, vertebrate
3. evolution, parasite
4. microscope, organism
5. anatomy, heredity
6. instinct

C.

1. chlorophyll
2. bacilli
3. protoplasm, carbohydrate
4. chromosome
5. catarrh
6. adenoids, laryngitis
7. allergy, antiseptic

D.

1. virus, vaccine
2. antibiotics
3. diagnosis, obstetrics
4. pediatrician
5. hormone, eczema
6. vaccine, hemorrhage

E.

1. astigmatism
2. cardiology
3. inoculate, paralysis
4. epilepsy

Mastery Test: Chapter 16

A.

1. nuclear fission
2. cyclotron
3. amplifier, fidelity
4. cathode ray
5. cosmic rays
6. Supersonic
7. abacus, infinity
8. Electronics

B.

1. integer, decimal
2. numerator, denominator
3. quotient
4. circumference, angle, isosceles
5. hypotenuse
6. perpendicular

C.

1. jet propulsion
2. fissionable
3. Frequency modulation

Mastery Test: Chapter 17

A.

1. facade, baroque
2. Gothic
3. Romanesque
4. gargoyles
5. abutments
6. girders
7. Lancet, nave
8. rotunda

B.

1. Byzantine
2. colonnades
3. buttresses
4. corridor, mosaic
5. wainscot, veneer
6. trellis
7. cornice
8. cantilever

Mastery Test: Chapter 18

A.

1. anxiety
2. psychoanalysis, psychiatry
3. Oedipus complex, transference
4. repression, hysteria
5. claustrophobia, amnesia
6. senility

B.

1. psychosomatic
2. Paranoid
3. inhibitions
4. neurosis, psychosis
5. empirical
6. aptitude, intelligence
7. sublimation
8. rapport

C.

1. Judaism, Christianity, Bible
2. Buddhism, Mohammedanism
3. orthodox, sacrilegious, atheism, blasphemy, deity

D.

1. gospel
2. catechism
3. baptism
4. theology, parochial
5. Crucifixion
6. prophets, congregation, parable
7. disciple

E.

1. Existentialism
2. extrasensory

Mastery Test: Chapter 19

A.

1. ballet, choreography
2. arabesque, pirouette, entrechat
3. abstraction
4. Surrealism

5. gouache
6. chiaroscuro
7. Ceramic

B.

1. fugue, counterpoint
2. madrigal
3. symphony
4. rhapsody
5. atonality, dissonance
6. a cappella
7. cadence, staccato

C.

1. autobiography
2. novel, essay
3. comedy, tragedy
4. Realism, romanticism
5. Naturalism
6. classicism
7. satire

D.

1. bibliography, drama
2. picaresque, narrative
3. soliloquy
4. lyric
5. imagery
6. prologue, rhythm, rhyme

Mastery Test: Chapter 20

A.

1. garçon, entrée, en route
2. in extremis, corps, coup de grace

3. bon vivant, savoir faire, joie de vivre
4. Détente, vox populi, laissez faire, status quo

B.

1. nom de plume, incognito, camouflage
2. connoisseur, bas-relief, facade, bona fide
3. cause célèbre, corpus delicti, mal de mer, hors-d'oeuvre

C.

1. bourgeoisie, non sequiturs, faux pas
2. gourmand, gourmet
3. pièce de résistance, cuisine, ersatz
4. a priori, carte blanche, ad infinitum

D.

1. tête-à-tête, protégé, debut
2. per diem, pro rata
3. alma mater, cortege
4. verboten, gratis
5. debutante, extempore, zeitgeist, carpe diem

E.

1. blitzkrieg, in toto, au revoir
2. baton, tour de force
3. vis-à-vis, verbatim
4. in absentia, de facto
5. weltanschauung, belles lettres

F.

1. crèche, leitmotiv
2. gauche, ex officio
3. finis, auf Wiedersehen

Answers to Core Word Mastery Tests

Mastery Test: Core Word List #1

Part I

1. it's
2. too
3. they're
4. to
5. there
6. Its
7. lose
8. fourth
9. Really
10. separation
11. whether, weather
12. chose, choose
13. effective
14. affect, effect
15. personal, personnel
16. women
17. definite
18. occurring
19. existence
20. beliefs

Part II

1. occurred
2. existence
3. business
4. accommodate
5. to
6. Forty
7. occasion
8. Definitely
9. definition
10. to

Part III

1. occur
2. losing
3. receive
4. believe
5. busy
6. all right
7. achievement
8. separate
9. criticism
10. realize

Part II

1. governor, writing
2. interpretation, condemn
3. Marriage, beneficial, disastrous
4. thorough
5. benefit
6. prejudice
7. intelligent
8. experience
9. conscientious
10. controversial
11. acquaintance
12. performance
13. description
14. comparative
15. perform

Part III

1. exaggerate
2. Immediately
3. incidentally
4. noticeable
5. privilege
6. possession
7. acquaint
8. conscious
9. loneliness
10. necessary

Part IV

Then the athlete began to write. He knew that during this examination he would have to begin to interpret his material. The choice of one strand of evidence rather than another would reveal whether he had benefited from his teacher's efforts to show him how to think and write.

Mastery Test: Core Word List #2

Part I

1. *t* written
2. athletic
3. *r* surprise
4. *e* interest
5. shining
6. *n* government
7. *n* environment
8. similar
9. among
10. *n* beginning

Mastery Test: Core Word List #3

Part I

1. describe, profession
2. probably, controversy
3. incident, repetition
4. category, succeed
5. using, psychology

Part II

The lonely professor tried without success to search his conscience for an explanation of his feeling that he was useless. But no immediate answer was forthcoming. No useful guide led him to truth; no friend could recommend a potion that might possess special powers to help him.

Part III

1. led, lead
2. passed, past
3. advice, advise
4. sense, principle, principal
5. varies, various

Part IV

1. apparent
2. approach
3. heroes
4. imaginary
5. foreigners
6. pursue
7. prevalent
8. analyze
9. consistent
10. rhythm
11. Heroic
12. height
13. studying
14. imagination
15. heroine

Mastery Test: Core Word List #4

Part I

1. opponent
2. opinion
3. exercise
4. characterize
5. disappoint
6. appearance
7. preferred
8. procedure
9. imagine
10. difference
11. irrelevant
12. optimism
13. embarrass
14. prominent
15. foreign

Part II

1. Negro
2. tries, tried
3. refer, opinion
4. conceives, predominant
5. arising, proceeding

Part III

1. referred
2. conceivable
3. characteristic
4. convenience
5. efficiency
6. optimism
7. irritable
8. maintenance
9. considerably
10. guidance

Part IV

1. i. oppose
2. g. arise
3. d. different
4. e. efficiency
5. f. dominant
6. j. opportunity
7. a. convenient
8. b. independence
9. c. precede
10. h. character

Mastery Test: Core Word List #5

Part I

1. f. psychopathic
2. g. psychoanalysis
3. a. humor
4. i. tragedy
5. b. hypocrite
6. h. subtle
7. c. temperament
8. d. villain
9. j. summary
10. e. sophomore
6. hindrance
7. ridicule
8. Satire
9. summed
10. suppress

Part II

1. argument
2. original
3. humorous
4. Hypocrisy
5. philosophy

Part III

1. controlled
2. tyranny
3. aggressive
4. suppose
5. unusual
6. techniques
7. therefore
8. unusually
9. humorist
10. sergeants

Part IV

1. arguing, propagates, propaganda, ridiculous
2. together, origin, satirize

3. independent, prefers
4. irresistible, amicable
5. inveigh, seize
6. inveigled, Granny, resonant
7. seizure, auxiliary

Mastery Test: Core Word List #6

Part I

1. Academically
2. accessible
3. acceptance
4. acceptable
5. accidental
6. accidentally
7. basically
8. finally
9. fundamental
10. fundamentally

11. outrageous
12. Capitol
13. excess
14. challenge
15. speaking

Part II

1. decision
2. Academy
3. access
4. Christianity
5. *Britannica*
6. accident
7. across
8. excessive
9. curiosity
10. discipline

Part III

1. Britain
2. academic
3. Christian
4. Lengthening
5. basis
6. coming
7. Familiar
8. curious
9. disciples
10. accept
11. salable
12. frivolous
13. blamable
14. exceed
15. capital

Part IV

I have decided that your article doesn't have enough strength of conviction. Before accepting it, I should like you to increase its length, strengthen its style, and support its arguments more forcefully. When, for example, you're speaking of Christ, Buddha, Lao-Tse, etc., you need to draw clearer distinctions among them.

Mastery Test: Core Word List #7

Part I

1. friend
2. weird
3. atheist
4. chief
5. deceiver
6. field
7. financiers
8. gaiety
9. leisure
10. perceive
11. ceiling
12. view
13. yield
14. piece
15. relieve
16. feign
17. alien
18. cashier
19. proficient
20. mischief

Part II

1. Financially
2. leisurely
3. attendant
4. authoritative
5. before
6. Careless
7. knowledge
8. laboratory
9. livelihood
10. ninety
11. authority
12. careful
13. happiness
14. influential
15. liveliness

Part III

The author's friendliness entertained those in attendance at the lecture. A few in the audience were hesitant to ask questions, since they were truly quite ignorant of his use of symbols. However, he was good-natured and tolerant of their awkward manners. Had their lives been as involved as those of his fictional characters, however (none of whom would have attended lectures of any kind), even his liveliest manner would have failed to influence them. In truth, his characters seem to be dependent solely upon a sense of personal misery and failure. The author himself had been known to succumb to a similarly negative outlook—but not that night!

Mastery Test: Core Word List #8

Part I

1. carrying
2. carrier
3. desirability
4. extremely
5. accompanied
6. advantageous
7. applies
8. changeable
9. companies
10. countries

Part II

1. omitted
2. swimming
3. buried
4. transferred
5. parallel
6. connotes
7. accompanying
8. carried
9. counselor
10. sufficient

11. consummate
12. curable
13. dilettante
14. innuendo
15. Passage

Part III

1. particular
2. theories
3. stories

Part IV

Sometimes a newspaper editor will bury or omit a story—and the picture that accompanies it—that carries references that do not show his favorite theory to advantage. With avail, a council of his fellow editors often counsel him not to permit his prejudice to corrupt his judgment.

Mastery Test: Core Word List #9

Part I

1. e. alleviate
2. g. stabilization
3. a. concede
4. j. allotment
5. c. accurate
6. f. amateur
7. b. sponsor
8. h. susceptible
9. d. aggravate
10. i. significance

Part II

1. continuous
2. paid
3. physical
4. undoubtedly
5. Accuracy
6. admittance
7. allotted
8. Tomorrow
9. tremendous
10. warrant

4. sincerely
5. connotation
6. changing
7. applying
8. accompaniment
9. desire
10. company
11. malicious
12. commissioner
13. scissors
14. strictly
15. recognize

11. crises
12. demonstrable
13. plausible
14. medicinal
15. stigma

Part III

1. planned
2. pleasant
3. possible
4. quantity
5. accomplish
6. admission
7. afraid
8. allowed
9. religion
10. response
11. ignoble
12. medieval
13. allocate
14. crisis
15. deplorable

Part IV

The minister left the altar for the pulpit. Those who thought he might make a speech of vengeance against sin did not accurately know their man. "I admit weakness in myself," he began. "He who allows it in himself must surely allow it in others."

Mastery Test: Core Word List #10
Part I

1. already, quiet
2. Altogether, all together
3. cite, device
4. due, except
5. hear, here
6. ingenious, later
7. loss, loose
8. moral, morale
9. prophesy, peace, prophecy
10. whole, scene

Part II

1. j. disillusioned
2. e. anticipate
3. a. symbol
4. b. accuser
5. h. calendar
6. d. annual
7. c. adolescent
8. i. dilemma
9. g. permanent
10. f. apology

Part III

1. morally
2. accuses
3. Adolescence
4. Annually
5. brilliant
6. cigarette
7. correlate
8. difficult
9. off
10. whose

Part IV

Having concluded his latest phase—accusing all his friends of faithlessness—Gerard apologized, explaining that he never knew where the source of his moods was. And, furthermore, he added, a man of his brilliance ought not be held accountable for mere rudeness, whether in discussing the amount of a bill or the character of the guests assembled at the dining table. Everyone simply concluded that Gerard was basically irascible.

Mastery Test: Core Word List #11

Part I

1. c. abundance
2. e. acclaim
3. f. adequate
4. i. cemetery
5. d. advertising
6. h. competition
7. j. genius
8. g. huge
9. b. hundred
10. a. apparatus

6. competitor
7. divide
8. escape
9. idea
10. medicine

Part II

1. Absence
2. abundant
3. adequately
4. advertiser
5. appreciate

Part III

1. accustom
2. actually
3. advertisement
4. children
5. hoping
6. dissatisfied
7. especially
8. literature
9. presence
10. eighth

Part IV

1. To succeed, a musical comedy must provide entertainment. During the show, the actors must seem to enjoy themselves; they must deliver lines to one another easily and naturally; every moment must suggest that this play is the finished product of months of actual practice and rehearsal. Maybe then the play will flourish, even if the soprano's voice is not divine.

2. The politician in my area is a plausible fellow of high presence. He has dropped mighty words about public safety and laid several cornerstones. But in actuality, he has dealt with no significant issue; he has, in brief, proved himself to be a hopeless incompetent.

Mastery Test: Core Word List #12

Part I

1. elicit
2. glacier
3. misshapen
4. liquefy
5. buoyant
6. dissonance

7. illusion
8. climactic
9. irrigate
10. sovereign
11. civilian
12. expatriate

13. stationery
14. panicked
15. collegiate

Part II

1. *i* gratuitous
2. disgress
3. mishap
4. *k* picnicking
5. divulge
6. *e* peaceable
7. fiend
8. *g* aggrandize
9. priestly
10. *e* mystery

Part III

1. admirable
2. slain
3. transient
4. wield
5. college
6. facetious
7. chastise
8. mysterious
9. skein
10. reducible
11. tier
12. imbibe
13. sleigh
14. illiterate
15. fierce

Part IV

When the passionate young Romero first saw the lovely mien of Lulu, Cupid's arrow flew straight to his pounding heart. She slew him with her fiery eyes. He proclaimed to have never met such kissable lips. But although Romero was persistent and likable, Lulu was immovable. She was a virtuoso of the cold shoulder and the waxen expression.

Mastery Test: Core Word List #13

Part I

1. competent, infallible
2. gaiety, chateau
3. ignite, erotic
4. embargo, Pier
5. extravagant, surfeit
6. intangible, visible
7. species, hierarchy
8. guardian, sobriety
9. erratic, predictable
10. martial, invincible

Part II

1. chocolate
2. receipt
3. omniscient
4. ingenuous
5. supplanted
6. shriek
7. serviceable
8. dwindling
9. diffident
10. interference

Part III

1. My neighbor was in such despair from the adverse circumstances of his life that he cut his veins with a razor. His face was so ashen I thought he might die, but Fate gave him a

reprieve. He is currently a patient at the state mental hospital.

2. The desert sun was sizzling down on the sheik's shabby tent. By inference, one might conclude he was living a subsistence existence, but such was not the case. The sheik was a munificent desert lord who lived in opulence.

3. A reference book is only as efficacious as it is usable. However, a systematic study of most texts proffering this kind of assistance shows that few qualify. It's a heinous crime against scholarship!

Core Word Pre-Test

1. losing
2. proceed
3. height
4. opinion
5. writing
6. professor
7. therefore
8. foreign
9. marriage
10. all right, alright
11. heroes
12. referred
13. amateur
14. atheist
15. ninety
16. advertisement
17. leisure
18. laboratory
19. irresistible
20. description
21. efficient
22. rhythm
23. embarrass
24. environment
25. exaggerate
26. prevalent
27. irrelevant
28. occurrence
29. accidentally
30. adolescence
31. weird
32. advantageous
33. parallel
34. immediately
35. beneficial
36. criticism
37. occasion
38. loneliness
39. characteristic
40. belief
41. accommodate
42. disappoint
43. grammar
44. athlete
45. interest
46. controversial
47. separate
48. maintenance
49. argument
50. villain

Core Word Post-Test

Part I

1. losing
2. proceed
3. height
4. opinion
5. writing
6. professor
7. therefore
8. foreign
9. marriage
10. all right, alright
11. heroes
12. referred
13. amateur
14. atheist
15. ninety
16. advertisement
17. leisure
18. laboratory
19. irresistible
20. description
21. efficient
22. rhythm
23. embarrass
24. environment
25. exaggerate
26. prevalent
27. irrelevant
28. occurrence
29. accidentally
30. adolescence
31. weird
32. advantageous
33. parallel
34. immediately
35. beneficial
36. criticism
37. occasion
38. loneliness
39. characteristic
40. belief
41. accommodate
42. disappoint
43. grammar
44. athlete
45. interest
46. controversial
47. separate
48. maintenance
49. argument
50. villain

Part II

1. admirable
2. alien
3. auxiliary
4. averse
5. bier
6. brief
7. Briton
8. cashier
9. ceiling
10. civilian
11. climactic
12. counterfeit
13. courageous
14. crotchet
15. deceitful
16. deign
17. deprecate
18. desirable
19. duly
20. either
21. elicit
22. exceed
23. excess
24. facetious
25. feign
26. fiend
27. fierce
28. fiery
29. gaiety
30. glacier
31. grief
32. likable
33. medieval
34. mien
35. mischief
36. movable
37. neighbor
38. neither
39. outrageous
40. patient
41. peaceable
42. picnicking
43. pier
44. proficient
45. reprieve
46. seizure
47. sleigh
48. straight
49. trolley
50. panicked

Comprehensive Word List

Core Words, Special Terms

a cappella
à la carte
abacus
abandonment
absence
abstraction
abundance
abundant
abutment
academic
academically
academy
accept
acceptable
acceptance
access
accessible
accessory
accident
accidental
accidentally
acclaim
accommodate
accompanies
accompaniment
accompanying
accomplish
accountant

accuracy
accurate
accurately
accuser
accusing
accustom
achieve
achievement
acknowledgment
acquaint
acquaintance
across
actual
actuality
actually
adenoids
adequate
adequately
adjudicate
admirable
admission
admit
admittance
adolescence
adolescent
advantage
advantageous
advertisement

advertiser
advertising
advice
advise
affect
affidavit
afraid
against
aggrandize
aggravate
aggressive
agreeable
alcohol
algebra
alibi
alien
alimony
all right
all together
allergy
alleviate
allocate
allotment
allotted
allow
alma mater
already
altar

altogether
amateur
amen
amicable
amnesia
among
amount
amphibian
amplifier
analysis
analyze
anatomy
angle
annual
annually
annul
another
antibiotics
anticipate
antihistamine
antiseptic
antitoxin
anxiety
apologized
apology
apparatus
apparent
appear

appearance
applies
applying
appreciate
approach
aptitude
arabesque
area
arguing
argument
arise
arising
arraign
article
ashen
astigmatism
atheism
atheist
athlete
athletic
atonality
attendance
attendant
attended
auditor
author
authoritative
authority
autobiography
auxiliary
averse

bacilli
bailiff
balcony
ballet
bandit
bankrupt
baptism
barbiturate
baroque
basically
basis
bazaar
before
began
begin
beginning
belief

believe
beneficial
benefit
benefited
Bible
bibliography
bigamy
blamable
blasphemy
blitzkrieg
bona fide
boomerang
botany
bourgeoisie
brilliance
brilliant
Britain
Britannica
Buddhism
buoyant
burglary
buried
bury
business
busy
buttress
Byzantine

caddy
cadence
calendar
camouflage
canary
cantilever
canyon
capital
capitol
carbohydrate
cardiology
careful
careless
carnivorous
carried
carrier
carrying
carte blanche
cashier
catarrh
catechism

category
cathode ray
cause célèbre
ceiling
cemetery
ceramic
challenge
changeable
changing
character
characteristic
characterize
chastise
chateau
cherub
chess
chiaroscuro
chief
children
chintz
chlorophyll
chocolate
choice
choose
choreography
chose
Christ
Christian
Christianity
chromosome
cigarette
circumference
cite
civilian
classicism
claustrophobia
climactic
coercion
coffee
collateral
college
collegiate
colonnade
comedy
coming
commissioner
companies
company
comparative

competent
competition
competitor
concede
conceivable
conceive
condemn
confetti
congregation
connoisseur
connotation
connote
conscience
conscientious
conscious
consider
considerably
consistency
consistent
consummate
continuous
contraband
control
controlled
controversial
controversy
convenience
convenient
coolie
cornice
corps
corral
correlate
corridor
cosmic ray
council
counsel
counselor-at-law
counselor
counterpoint
countries
coup de grace
coupon
coyote
crises
crisis
criticism
criticize
crucifixion

cuisine
curable
curiosity
curious
cyclotron
czar

dealt
debut
debutante
deceitful
deceive
decided
decimal
decision
defendant
define
definite
definitely
definition
deity
demonstrable
denominator
dependent
deplorable
describe
description
desirability
desirable
desire
despair
détente
device
diagnosis
difference
different
difficult
diffident
digress
dilemma
dilettante
dining
disappoint
disastrous
disciple
discipline
disillusioned
dissatisfied
dissimilar

dissonance
ditto
divan
divide
divine
divulge
doesn't
dominant
drama
dropped
due
dunning
during
dwindling

easily
eczema
effect
effective
efficacious
efficiency
efficient
eighth
electronics
elicit
elite
embargo
embarrass
embezzle
embryo
empirical
entertain
entertainment
entrechat
entrée
entrepreneur
environment
epilepsy
erotic
erratic
ersatz
escape
especially
essay
etc.
every
evolution
exaggerate
exceed

except
excess
excessive
exercise
exist
existence
existent
existentialism
expatriate
experience
explanation
extrasensory
extravagant
extremely

facade
facetious
familiar
faux pas
feign
fez
fidelity
field
fiend
fierce
fiery
finally
financially
financier
fissionable
flotilla
foreign
foreigners
forty
fourth
franchise
frequency modulation
friend
friendliness
frivolous
fugue
fulfill
fundamental
fundamentally
fungus
further

gaiety
garbage

garçon
gargoyle
genius
gingham
girder
glacier
gong
gospel
Gothic
gouache
gourmand
gourmet
government
governor
grammar
gratis
gratuitous
guardian
guidance
gusto
gypsy

happiness
hear
height
heinous
hemorrhage
here
heredity
hero
heroes
heroic
heroine
hesitant
hierarchy
hindrance
homicide
hopeless
hoping
horde
hormone
hors-d'oeuvre
huge
hull
humor
humorist
humorous
hundred
hypertension

hypocrisy
hypocrite
hypotenuse
hysteria

idea
ignite
ignoble
illiterate
illusion
imagery
imaginary
imagination
imagine
imbibe
immediate
immediately
immovable
incident
incidentally
incognito
independence
independent
indictment
indigo
infallible
inference
infinity
influence
influential
ingenious
ingenuous
inhibition
innuendo
inoculate
instinct
intangible
integer
intelligence
intelligent
interest
interference
interpret
interpretation
inveigh
inveigle
invincible
involve
irascible

irrelevant
irresistible
irrigate
irritable
isosceles
it's
its

jackal
jet propulsion
joie de vivre
jubilee
Judaism

ketchup (catsup)
khaki
kindergarten
kissable
knowledge

laboratory
laid
laissez-faire
lancet
laryngitis
lasso
later
lead
led
ledger
leisure
leisurely
length
lengthening
liability
likable
liquefy
liquidate
literature
liveliest
livelihood
liveliness
lives
loneliness
lonely
loose
lose
losing
lyric

madrigal
maintenance
malicious
mammal
management
marriage
martial
maybe
medicinal
medicine
medieval
merchandise
mere
meter (metre)
microscope
mien
mischief
mishap
misshapen
Mohammedanism
moral
morale
morally
mortgage
mosaic
mosquito
munificent
mysterious
mystery

nadir
narrative
nave
necessary
negotiable
Negro
Negroes
neighbor
neurosis
ninety
noticeable
novel
nuclear fission
numerator

oasis
obstetrics
occasion
occur

occurred
occurrence
occurring
Oedipus complex
off
omit
omitted
omniscient
operate
opinion
opponent
opportunity
oppose
optimism
opulence
organism
origin
original
orthodox
outrageous

paid
pajama
panicked
parable
parallel
paralysis
paranoid
parasite
parochial
particular
passage
passed
past
patient
peace
peaceable
peccadillo
pediatrician
penicillin
per diem
perceive
perform
performance
permanent
permit
perpendicular
persistent
persona non grata

personal
personnel
phase
philosophy
physical
picaresque
picnicking
piece
pièce de résistance
pier
pirouette
planned
plausible
pleasant
politician
possess
possession
possible
practice
precede
predictable
predominant
prefer
preferred
prejudice
presence
prevalent
priestly
principal
principle
privilege
probably
procedure
proceed
profession
professor
proffering
proficient
prologue
prominent
promissory
propaganda
propagate
prophecy
prophet
protégé
protoplasm
psychiatry
psychoanalysis

psychology
psychopathic
psychosis
psychosomatic
pursue

qualify
quantity
quiet
quotient

ranch
rapport
realism
realize
really
receipt
receive
receiving
recognize
recommend
reducible
refer
reference
referred
referring
relieve
religion
renegade
repetition
repression
reprieve
resonant
response
rhapsody
rhyme
rhythm
ridicule
ridiculous
Romanesque
romanticism
rotunda

Sabbath
sacrilegious
safety
salable
salvo
satire

satirize
savoir faire
scene
scissors
seize
seizure
senility
sense
sentence
separate
separation
sergeant
sheik
shining
shriek
significance
similar
sincerely
sizzling
skein
skipper
slain
sleigh
slew
sloop
sobriety
soliloquy
sophomore
source
sovereign
soy
speaking
species
speech
sponsor
stabilization
staccato
stationery
status quo
stigma
stories
story
strafe
straight
strength
streptomycin
strictly
studying
sublimation

subpoena
subsistence
subtle
succeed
success
succotash
succumb
sufficient
summary
summed
supersonic
supplant
suppose
suppress
surfeit
surprise
surrealism
susceptible
swimming
symbol
symphony
syndicate
systematic

taboo
tariff
tattoo
technique
temperament
tête-à-tête
than
their
themselves
then
theology
theories
theory
there
therefore
they're
thorough
those
thought
tier
to
tobacco
together
tolerant
tomato

tomorrow
too
tornado
tragedy
transference
transferred
transient
trellis
tremendous
tried
tries
two
tyranny

undoubtedly
unusual
unusually

usable
useful
useless
using
usury

vaccine
vampire
varies
various
vein
vendetta
veneer
vengeance
verbatim
verboten
vertebrate

view
villain
virtuoso
virus
vis-à-vis
visible

wainscot
waltz
warrant
waxen
weather
weird
weltanschauung
where
whether
whole

whose
wield
woman
women
writ
write
writer
writing
written

yield
you're

zeitgeist
zenith
zoology